Francis Burke Brandt

Friedrich Eduard Beneke

The Man and his Philosophy

Francis Burke Brandt

Friedrich Eduard Beneke
The Man and his Philosophy

ISBN/EAN: 9783337079451

Printed in Europe, USA, Canada, Australia, Japan

Cover: Foto ©ninafisch / pixelio.de

More available books at **www.hansebooks.com**

FRIEDRICH EDUARD BENEKE

THE MAN AND HIS PHILOSOPHY

AN INTRODUCTORY STUDY

BY

FRANCIS BURKE BRANDT, A. B.

SUBMITTED IN PARTIAL FULFILMENT OF THE REQUIREMENTS
FOR THE DEGREE OF DOCTOR OF PHILOSOPHY
IN THE
UNIVERSITY FACULTY OF PHILOSOPHY
COLUMBIA COLLEGE

NEW YORK
MAY, 1895

INTRODUCTORY NOTE

WHILE the following work in form is in no sense deliberately polemic, it will be found in spirit to contain as its underlying thought the contention that, if German idealistic philosophy is to be regarded as a systematic development, the true development after Kant is to be found, not in Fichte, Schelling and Hegel, but in the philosophical system of Friedrich Eduard Beneke. This is only to say in other words that in the philosophy of Beneke we have both in outcome and in method the profoundest metaphysical insight of our century. While this may seem a bold claim on behalf of a philosopher comparatively obscure, it is believed that the evidence of the following pages will justify the assertion. The reasons for Beneke's accidental obscuration are there set forth. That this has not been due to the inherent deficiency of Beneke's system, is also amply proved by the progressively increasing recognition of its significance and importance on the part of German historians of philosophy. For example, in the earlier histories, as Schwegler's (Stuttgart, 1847), E. Reinhold's (Jena, 1854), Beneke is not even mentioned. In more recent works, like those of Erdmann and Windelband, he is practically neglected and his significance unappreciated. It is therefore significant that in a most recent German history of philosophy,[1] not only is

[1] Bergmann: *Geschichte der Philosophie*, Berlin, 1893. 2 vols. (Vol. II.: *Die deutsche Philosophie von Kant bis Beneke*.) This work first fell into the hands of the writer just as the present volume was going to press.

German philosophy made to end with Beneke, but in a work which assigns forty pages to Hegel, Beneke is given an equal space.

It may be added that the following pages do not pretend to give a full presentation of Beneke's views in their coercive completeness. Beneke's philosophical system is too extended to be brought with convincing force into so narrow a compass. This work therefore hopes to serve chiefly as an introductory statement which may prove of value both in exhibiting the spirit and significance of the system, and in stimulating to such further study as may result not merely in a juster appreciation of a neglected man, but also in a truer conception of metaphysical truth.

CONTENTS

PART I—THE MAN

CHAPTER I

	PAGE
EARLY LIFE AND OPENING CAREER	15–25
I. *Boyhood and Early Education*	15
II. *Interdiction, and Sojourn at Göttingen*	18

CHAPTER II

LIFE ACTIVITY AT BERLIN	26–37
I. *Intellectual Development*	26
(1) Formative Philosophical Influences	26
(2) Relation to Kant.	28
(a) Critic of the Kantian Philosophy	28
(b) Pioneer of "the Movement back to Kant."	29
II. *Life Effort and Literary Activity*	31
(1) Opposition to the Philosophical Tendencies of the Times	31
(2) Lectures and Writings.	33
III. *Character*	36

PART II—THE PHILOSOPHY

CHAPTER I

HISTORICAL BASIS AND THEORY OF KNOWLEDGE 38–52
- § 1. General Introduction 38
- I. *Doctrines of Perception before Kant*. 40
  - § 2. Shortcomings of Earlier Doctrines 40
- II. *The Kantian Theory* 41
  - § 3. General Character of the Problem 41
  - § 4. Aim of the Kantian Philosophy 43
  - § 5. The Kantian Theory Stated by Beneke . . . 44
  - § 6. Kantian Distinction of Knowledge Independent of Experience 45
  - § 7. Beneke's Criticism of this Theory 47
  - § 8. Resolution of the Inherent Contradiction of the Kantian Theory 49
  - § 9. Internal Sense Yields Knowledge of a Thing in Itself 50
  - § 10. Permanent Value of the Kantian Analysis . . 51

CHAPTER II

BENEKE'S SYSTEM IN GENERAL OUTLINE 53–71
- I. *The Scope and Method of Psychology* 53
  - § 11. Starting Point of Empirical Psychology . . . 53
  - § 12. Subject Matter of Empirical Psychology . . . 54
  - § 13. Psychology as Distinguished from Outer Sciences 55
  - § 14. The Method of Psychology 55
- II. *The Relation of Soul and Body* 55
  - § 15. The Method of Natural Science is Not Materialism 55
  - § 16. Opposition of Soul and Body One in and for Consciousness 56
  - § 17. Psychical and Corporeal Processes Likewise Distinctions for Consciousness 57
  - § 18. The Real Relation between Soul and Body . . 58

		PAGE
III.	*The Origin of Consciousness*	60
	§ 19. Meaning of "Origin of Consciousness."	60
	§ 20. Metaphysical Method of Solution	60
	§ 21. Psychological Method of Solution	62
	§ 22. Source of the Notion that Self-Consciousness is Materially Conditioned	64
IV.	*The Unity of Mind or Consciousness*	65
	§ 23. Beneke Compared with English and with German Thinkers	65
	§ 24. The Soul as a Hierarchy of Faculties	66
	§ 25. The Soul as a "Simple," or Abstract Unity	67
	§ 26. The Soul as a Concrete Psychical Organism	70

CHAPTER III

BENEKE'S EMPIRICAL PSYCHOLOGY—INTRODUCTION 72–86

I.	*Psychology as a Natural Science*	72
	§ 27. Introduction	72
	§ 28. Inner Experience the Immediate Object of Psychology	72
	§ 29. The Objective Method Dealing with the Inner Experience of Others	73
	§ 30. The Subjective Method Dealing with the Experience of One's Own Self	74
	§ 31. Possibility of Applying the Method of the External Sciences to Inner Experience	74
II.	*General Nature of the Psychological Problem*	76
	§ 32. The Problem Stated	76
	§ 33. Previous Attempts at Solution	76
	§ 34. The Problem as Conceived by Beneke	81
III.	*Beneke's Doctrine of Traces*	82
	§ 35. Transition	82
	§ 36. The Fact of Psychical Persistence and How Known	82
	§ 37. Nature of Unconscious Persistence	84
	§ 38. The Philosophical Significance of Memory	85

CHAPTER IV

THE PSYCHOLOGY OF INNER EXPERIENCE 87–110
  I. *General Introduction* 87
    § 39. Transition 87
    § 40. Knowledge both Product and Process 87
    § 41. Changes *to* Consciousness and Changes *in* Consciousness 88
  II. *Inner Experience: Origin of Individual Facts* 89
    § 42. The Facts of Inner Experience 89
    § 43. The Origin and Growth of Ideas 89
        (1) Memories 90
        (2) Concepts 91
        (3) Judgments 92
        (4) Inferences 93
    § 44. First Fundamental Psychological Process . . 94
  III. *Inner Experience: A Continuous Process of Redistribution* 95
    § 45. Introduction 95
    § 46. Alteration in Inner Experience a Change in Activity 95
    § 47. Beneke's Doctrine of "Movable Elements." . . 96
    § 48. Immediately Active Inner Consciousness the Resultant of a Dynamic Process 98
    § 49. Why Forms Immediately Present in Inner Consciousness become Inactive 100
    § 50. Second Fundamental Psychological Process . . 101
  IV. *Inner Experience: An Association of Ideas* 101
    § 51. Introduction 101
  A.—THE CONNECTIONS BETWEEN IDEAS 102
    § 52. Nature of the Problem 102
    § 53. Nature of the Union between Like Psychical Forms 102
    § 54. Effect of Conscious Activity on the Inner Character of the Trace 103
    § 55. Effect of the Inner Character of the Trace on Active Consciousness 105

§ 56. Laws of Quantitative Differences of Presentations 106
§ 57. Nature of the Union between Unlike Psychical Forms 106
§ 58. Connections between Conscious Forms Strengthened by Repetition 108
B.—DIRECTION FOLLOWED IN THE TRANSFERENCE OF CONSCIOUS ACTIVITY 109
§ 59. Law of the Direction of Consciousness . . . 109
§ 60. The Law Applied to the Old Laws of Association. 109

CHAPTER V

THE PSYCHOLOGY OF OUTER EXPERIENCE 111–120
§ 61. Introduction 111
I. *Outer Experience: Origin and Growth of Percepts* . . 111
§ 62. Fundamental Characteristics of the Perceptive Consciousness 111
§ 63. The Origin of Sense-Perceptions 112
§ 64. Sense-Perceptions as Products of Subjective and Objective Factors 113
§ 65. Nature and Meaning of "Original Sense-Impressions." 114
§ 66. Significance of Original Minimal Sensations as Inevitable Hypotheses 115
§ 67. Beneke's Doctrine of Primary Powers 116
§ 68. Third Fundamental Psychological Process . . 117
II. *Outer Experience: Objective Relations of Percepts* . . 117
§ 69. Introduction 117
§ 70. Nature of the Problem 118
§ 71. Objective Relations Depend on Original Organic Relations of the Primary Powers 118
§ 72. Objective and Subjective Connections Distinguished 120

CHAPTER VI

CONCLUSIONS RELATING TO BOTH INNER AND OUTER CONSCIOUS
EXPERIENCE 121–139
  I. *The Character and Kinds of Active Consciousness* . . 121
    § 73. Character of Consciousness as Determined by
        Methods of Excitation 121
    § 74. The Nature of Voluntary Action 122
    § 75. Character of Consciousness as Determined by
        Kinds of Primary Powers 123
    § 76. Immediate Consciousness as Determined by the
        Relation of Power and Stimulant 124
    § 77. The Threefold Nature of Consciousness . . . 125
 II. *The Span of Immediate Consciousness* 126
    § 78. Introduction 126
    § 79. The Span of Inner Consciousness 126
    § 80. The Span of Outer Consciousness 128
    § 81. The Relation between Sleeping and Waking . 129
    § 82. Why the Activity of Various Systems Monopolizes Immediate Consciousness 129
    § 83. Fourth Fundamental Psychological Process . . 131
III. *The Nature and Meaning of Consciousness* 132
    § 84. Introduction 132
  A.—CONSCIOUSNESS AS PRESENTED CONTENTS 132
    § 85. Consciousness Distinguished as Presented Contents 132
    § 86. Grades of Clearness of Presented Contents . . 133
    § 87. "Unconsciousness" Distinguished as (1) Less
        Clear, and as (2) Non-presented Contents. 134
  B.—CONSCIOUSNESS AS PRESENTATIVE PROCESS 136
    § 88. Consciousness Distinguished as Presentative
        Activity 136
    § 89. Clear Consciousness as a Grade of Presentative
        Activity 136
    § 90. Grades of Presentative Activity 138
    § 91. "Unconsciousness" Distinguished as Non-excitation 139

CHAPTER VII

PAGE

APPLIED PSYCHOLOGY—METAPHYSICS 140–156
    § 92. Introduction 140
  I. *The Original Nature and Being of the Soul* 141
    § 93. Psychological Summary of the Nature of the Soul 141
    § 94. Unity of Consciousness Distinguished from Unity of Being 142
    § 95. The Soul a Concrete Psychical Organism . . . 143
  II. *The Nature and Limits of Knowledge* 144
    § 96. The Intuition of Self 144
    § 97. The Origin and Content of "Inner Sense." . 145
    § 98. The Soul the Only Being Known In Itself. . . 147
  III. *Knowledge of Beings Other than Self* 148
    § 99. Fundamental Starting Point 148
    § 100. How Knowledge of the Existence of Other Beings is Attained 148
    § 101. The Being of Other Men 150
    § 102. The Being of Material Things 151
    § 103. The External World, So Far as Concerns Our Fellow-Beings, Neither Unknown Nor Unknowable 152
  IV. *God and Immortality* 153
    § 104. Introduction 153
    § 105. The Existence of God 153
    § 106. Immortality 154

CONCLUDING CHAPTER

  I. Brief Critical Estimate 157
  II. Permanent Influence and Followers 161
  III. Bibliography 164

Part I

The Man

Chapter I

Early Life and Opening Career

THE life of Friedrich Eduard Beneke naturally divides into two important periods. The first period includes the early life and career of Beneke up to the close of his sojourn at Göttingen, where after the interdiction of his early lectures at Berlin he found a welcome refuge. The second period begins with his return to Berlin, where the remainder of his long career was spent in active work at the great University. The present chapter is concerned with the first period.

I BOYHOOD AND EARLY EDUCATION

Beneke had the privilege of spending his boyhood days under the kindly eyes of his parents at Berlin, where on February 17th, 1798, he was born. His father was a Commissioner of Justice and Attorney-General. His mother was the sister of a preacher named Wilmsen, well known as the writer of stories for young people. No particular facts relating to either father or mother seem extant, but of the uncle it is said that his stimulating nature was not without permanent influence on the later life of the young Beneke.

In his early education Beneke had the advantage of the

best schools at Berlin. So rapidly did he advance in his preparatory studies that by his twelfth year he was ready to enter the upper third class of the Friedrich Werner Gymnasium, then under the direction of Bernhardi. Here he showed earnest love of study and developed a marked interest in mathematics. His versatility, however, went much farther. It extended to metrical translations of the classical poets, as well as to the production of some original poetic flights. Both of these performances made him known among his associates as "the poet." During this period, too, he developed a keen interest in gymnastic exercises and outdoor sports. This resulted in a vigorousness of body that served him in good stead, when, in 1815, he left school to enlist as a volunteer in the German war of independence.

The war having ended, Beneke, at Easter, 1816, began his university career with the study of theology at Halle. Here he came under the influence of the theologians Knapp and Gesenius. So successful was he in his theological studies that he twice gained a prize of honor. His interest at this time was to no small degree philosophical also, and this interest it was, perhaps, that brought him back the following year to Berlin. The young theologian then took his first examinations, and in order to qualify himself for practical work, became a hearer of the best pulpit orators in Berlin, among whom was Schleiermacher, whose church every Sunday was the assembling place of the most cultivated church-goers. It was while attending these discourses that the young theologian first became clearly conscious of his true mission. "That was," says Dr. Schmidt, "to open up a new path in the province of philosophy."[1] This insight into the nature of his mission was doubtless partly the result of Schleiermacher's stimulation, and partly the result of the searching conversations which Beneke was accustomed to hold with

[1] *Pädagogisches Jahrbuch für 1856*, p. 8.

his brother, as the two wended their way to hear the great preacher. At any rate, this mission became at this time the resolution of his life, and the following two years were spent in active preparation for his work.

In the winter of 1820, Beneke began as *privat docent*, his first lectures at the University of Berlin. In his inaugural dissertation, *De veris philosophiæ initiis*, he struck the keynote of the "pioneer movement" which he contemplated. This new philosophical standpoint had indeed already been indicated in two small works,[2] previously published this year, but in the inaugural it was, as Dressler says, still "more clearly demonstrated." The new standpoint contended for in the three works mentioned, questioned most deeply the matter of philosophical method, and the prevailing theory of knowledge. As to the first point, in its declarations against the *a priori* method it was most emphatic, setting over against this method a purely empirical one, and holding that the fundamental basis for all knowledge must be experience— inner experience. This was directed in part against the Kantian *a priori* "forms" of knowledge, in part against the prevailing attempt to reach a knowledge of the absolute deductively. As to the second point, it criticised sharply the Kantian doctrine of the "internal sense," which regarded this form of experience as also phenomenal, and so as yielding no absolute knowledge of the Soul or Ego in itself. In opposition to this, it enunciated the important principle that in inner experience we gain absolute knowledge of a thing in itself, and that thing the soul. Or, to put it in the words of Falckenberg, who has most compactly and clearly summarized Beneke's position as set forth in these works:

[2] Outlines of the Theory of Knowledge (*Erkenntnisslehre nach dem Bewusstsein der reinen Vernunft in ihren Grundzügen dargelegt*, Jena, *1820*).
Empirical Psychology as the Basis of all Knowlege (*Erfahrungsseelenlehre als Grundlage alles Wissens in ihren Hauptzügen dargestellt*, Berlin, 1820).

"The root and basis of all knowledge is experience; metaphysics is itself an empirical science; it is the last in the series of philosophical disciplines. Whoever begins with metaphysics, instead of ending with it, begins the house at the roof. The point of departure for all cognition is inner experience or self-observation; hence the fundamental science is psychology, and all other branches of philosophy nothing but applied psychology. By the inner sense we perceive our ego as it really is, not merely as it appears to us; the only object whose *per se* we immediately know is the soul; in self-consciousness being and representation are one."[3]

When it is remembered that the prevailing philosophy at Berlin at this time was that of Hegel, and that the influence of Fichte had by no means yet passed away, one is able to appreciate the Herculean task to which Beneke, nothing daunted, had set himself. But the young twenty-four-year-old *privat docent* soon found that his real difficulties were to come not from a fair and inherent conflict of thought with thought, in which truth would be given opportunity to prevail, but from personal and preconceived opposition, backed by the keen edge of governmental authority.

II INTERDICTION AND SOJOURN AT GÖTTINGEN

Early in the summer of 1822, Beneke's lectures at Berlin were brought to a sudden close. Notice was sent that during the comming summer semester his lectures must not be continued. Beneke was astounded. With a good deal of persistence, he sought again and again from the authorities some explanation of the interdiction, but in vain. Finally he appealed to the government. At last, to one of the many remonstrances made by him, he received from Minister Von

---

[3] Falckenberg, *History of Modern Philosophy* (tr. by A. C. Armstrong, New York, 1893), p. 510.

Altenstein, under date of March 5, 1822, a letter[1] in which it was stated that his recently published book, "Groundwork of the Physics of Morals," had caused some doubt as to his fitness to teach, and until some decision could be reached on this point, his lectures could not be received. Further, that the matter had been turned over to Chancellor Schultz, to whom he must apply for any further explanation. Many efforts were made to see Chancellor Schultz, but he was a hard man to get at. Finally, after a long delay, Beneke's uncle succeeded in getting a letter from him, dated July 15, 1822, in which he said that maturer investigation had only confirmed his originally hasty impression, viz.: that Minister Von Altenstein had sufficient reason to refuse Beneke's lectures. "In accordance with my duty and conscience," he writes, "I cannot therefore propose anything else than that henceforth permission to deliver philosophical discourses at this place continue denied to Dr. Beneke."[5]

One learns with a good deal of indignation of the efforts, official and personal, which were made to stifle the opposing thought of the promising young philosopher. There seems good reason for believing that these efforts were ultimately traceable to the influence of Hegel, whose overweening belief in the superiority of his own philosophical system had made him inimical even to the privilege of a hearing for an opposing thinker. While the ostensible cause for Beneke's exclusion from the University was his "Physics of Morals," and the formal objection to this was contained in the use of the term "Physics," back of this lay a far deeper reason, to which indeed this word "Physics" was the keynote. For Beneke had used the term as a sharp antithesis to "Metaphysics," meaning thereby to differentiate his own method

---

[1] Given in the *Pädagogisches Jahrbuch*, 1856, pp. 9-10.
[5] *Pädagogisches Jahrbuch*, 1856, p. 11. The letter is given in full.

from the metaphysical one of Kant, Fichte, Schelling, and Hegel. As a matter of fact, it was Beneke's intelligent opposition to this method that the government, under the influence of Hegel, endeavored to crush.

Ueberweg goes no further, it is true, than to say that "Beneke *pretended* to have discovered that this interdict resulted from the representations made by Hegel to his friend, Minister von Altenstein, and that Hegel's object was to prevent the propagation and reception at the University of Berlin of any philosophy hostile to his own and akin to the doctrine of Schleiermacher and Fries."[6] Falckenberg, however, expressly concedes[7] that Hegel was "unfavorably disposed toward" Beneke, and there seems to have been good ground for Beneke's belief. For that the opposition to him did not originate with the government, but had its source within the University, appears evidenced by the fact that Minister Von Altenstein, in his first letter to Beneke, tried to shift at least the complete explanation of the whole matter upon the shoulders of the University authorities, to whom Beneke was referred for "further explanation."[8] More than that, at the time when Beneke first received notice that his lectures were prohibited, and sought out the authorities for some cause, "A person somewhat important at the time," says Dr. Schmidt,[9] "who was approached by Beneke's anxious relatives for advice and help in behalf of the young man, whose whole career seemed blighted by the exclusion, advised them in confidence that he should, howsoever sour it might be for him, teach the Hegelian philosophy for a few years for appearance sake, so that later, when his place

---

[6] *History of Philosophy* (tr. by Morris, New York, 1888), Vol. II, p. 283.

[7] *History of Modern Philosophy*, p. 510.

[8] For this letter in full see *Pädagogisches Jahrbuch*, 1856, p. 10.

[9] Ibid., pp. 8-9.

seemed assured, he might gradually bend around again to his own system." One is not surprised to find Dr. Schmidt adding that Beneke "rejected this proposition with scorn." For he was more bent on ultimate truth than on the propagation of any system as system, even his own.

That the real source of the opposition to his lecturing was Hegelian, Beneke finally, after many written remonstrances, succeeded in wringing from Minister von Altenstein himself. "The Minister himself," says Dr. Schmidt, "repeatedly explained to Beneke in person that: 'No single proposition of his philosophy had given offence, but the whole of it; a philosophy which did not deduce everything from the absolute, which did not explain everything in relation to the absolute, was in general no philosophy, and could not be tolerated as philosophy.'"[10] Beneke was unable to refrain from giving vent to his opposite convictions; but his boldness in contradicting a philosophical doctrine supported by a Minister of State made matters only worse.[11]

Not satisfied with prohibiting his lectures at Berlin, Von Altenstein, "irritated," says Ueberweg, "by the further steps on the part of Beneke, found means to force the Saxon government, which had designated him for a regular professorship of Philosophy, not to appoint to that position a *privat docent*, from whom, although politically unsuspected, in Prussia the *Venia legendi* had been withdrawn."[12] The full

---

[10] *Pädagogisches Jahrbuch*, p 12.

[11] It is a matter of historical interest to compare this governmental aid to the Hegelian system with the return service of that system to the Government. On this point the judgment of Schwegler is interesting. In his *Handbook of the History of Philosophy* (tr. by Stirling, Edinburgh), speaking of Hegel after his call to Berlin, he says (p. 322), "Here too, he acquired from his connexion with the Prussian bureaucracy, as well politcal influence for himself, as the credit for his system of a State-philosophy : *not always to the advantage of the inner freedom of his philosophy, or of its moral worth.*"

[12] History, Vol. II, p. 283.

details of this persecution of Beneke are given by Dr. Schmidt in the biographical notice already referred to. It appears that the authorities at the University of Jena had already set their eyes on Beneke for a full professorship, and in November, 1822, wrote to Von Altenstein, asking whether a professorship in their University might be transferred to him. Beneke learned of the matter first in March, 1823. He then received a letter from General Superintendent Röhr, informing him of the affair, and saying that up to that time no answer had been received from the Minister.

The Saxon government had been forced to make this application to the government at Berlin, because of what Ueberweg calls the "forced interpretation" of "certain illiberal resolutions of the German Confederation." Ueberweg speaks as though this interpretation was made by Von Altenstein, although Dr. Schmidt says that it had been rendered to Röhr by "a person high in authority in Weimar."[13] This person had said to Röhr: "I should be very willing to help our Jena, and consequently Dr. Beneke; only I do not see how this is possible, as long as the anathema in Berlin is not withdrawn, or at least is not mitigated to us by an explanation. The prohibition of a *privat docent* to teach is the same as the removal of an officially appointed professor. We must assume—this much one goverment owes to another—that the royal Prussian government has acted for a cause, and in a legitimate way. And now, there is the familiar resolution of the Diet, steadfast adherence to which His Royal Highness the Grand Duke imposed upon us as our duty from the moment when it was settled as a resolution and a law of the Confederation. As usually the last, here the first word decides: 'An excluded teacher may not be reinstated by another confederated state in any public institution of learning.' '*Ita lex scripta est.*'" There was therefore nothing for

---

[13] *Pädagogisches Jahrbuch*, p. 12.

the authorities at Jena to do but first get permission of Von Altenstein to bring Beneke to Weimar. But their letter containing this request that honorable Minister had seen fit to ignore.

Shortly after the receipt of Superintendent Röhr's letter, Beneke applied to Minister Von Altenstein for a testimonial showing that there was no accusation against him which prevented his taking a situation abroad. Von Altenstein replied promptly, but this is what he said: "In reply to your memorial of the 5th inst., I hereby inform you that, although I have found myself obliged to prohibit entirely the continuance of your philosophical lectures at the University of this place, partly because, in consequence of your writings becoming known to me, in general I was not able to have confidence in the maturity of your insight, a thing which should distinguish the teacher of a philosophical discipline, partly because in particular I was obliged to criticize in you an onesidedness of consideration, which could easily have influenced to their great disadvantage young men who were to be introduced to the study of philosophy by you,—still, in other respects, I have found not the least thing to object either against your conduct or your sentiments."[14]

Of course such a "testimonial" not only absolutely prevented Beneke from getting the position at Jena, but tended to do him positive harm.

It is interesting to note, however, that this ministerial opinion was not shared at Jena. Von Altenstein had been so outspoken in his opinion that of course there was no alternative for the Saxon government; but Röhr, in a letter to Beneke, made very plain the feeling of disappointment at Jena over the outcome of the negotiations. In this letter, dated September 16, he further said: "Had not the ministerial testimonial given to you expressly said your philoso-

[14] *Pädagogisches Jahrbuch*, 1856, p. 13.

phy could easily influence to their detriment young students, one would perhaps easily have decided in your favor; but such decided suspicions, necessarily, in consideration of the circumstances, caused the *better private convictions* of our Ministry, *which were grounded on your writings*, to remain silent."[15] I have italicised some of the last few words to emphasize how Beneke's thought, considered in itself, was regarded by others.

Since, in very consequence of this deliberate and resolute attempt to stifle his philosophy, Beneke desired only the more to continue as a University teacher, he finally, in the beginning of the year 1824, repaired to Göttingen, where he remained for three years. Here his system grew rapidly under his facile pen, and as a result of his activity during this period,[16] we have two of his best works, the "Psychological Sketches," (*Psychologische Skizzen*),[17] in two volumes, and the "Relation of Soul and Body" (*Das Verhältniss von Seele und Leib*).

Dressler speaks in the highest praise of the *Skizzen*. He says: "These are no mere outlines of psychological science, but in them this knowledge is presented in complete detail, and one finds here a richness of psychological observation such as only a Beneke can supply. No nation has a like work which can bear comparison with it, and it is not too much to assert that in it we have the discovery of an entirely new world (the discovery of the inner world). What the feelings truly are, wherein they differ from the other activities of the soul, no one before Beneke's time was able to de-

---

[15] *Pädagogisches Jahrbuch*, p. 14.

[16] Before going to Göttingen, and while he was waiting for the removal of the dark cloud overhanging him, Beneke put forth two other works: "An Apology for my Groundwork of the Physics of Morals;" and "Contributions to a purely Psychological Theory of Psychological Pathology."

[17] These two volumes were first published separately under different titles.

termine; further, how consciousness arises, changes and raises itself to higher forms, likewise was first proven agreeable to nature by him * * ."[18]

Early in 1827 Beneke was given permission to resume his lectures at Berlin. "Whether," says Schmidt, "the latter (his system) had now gained authority alongside of others also in Berlin, or Beneke's significance itself had become more recognized, or one thought to make good to Beneke the neglect occasioned through misunderstanding—whatever it was, it happened that his earlier relations with the University of Berlin were restored, when, at Easter, 1827, he returned to Berlin, where his presence at that time was required by family circumstances."[19]

Beneke's later life in Berlin will be considered in the next chapter.

---

[18] *Kurze Charakteristik der Sämmtlichen Werke Beneke's*, p. 294. Given as an appendix to the fourth edition of Beneke's *Lehrbuch*, Berlin, 1877.

[19] *Pädagogisches Jahrbuch*, p. 15.

CHAPTER II

LIFE ACTIVITY AT BERLIN

WITH his return to the University of Berlin in 1827, Beneke began a long active career, which lasted till his death in 1854. In treating of this period I shall speak of his intellectual development, of his life effort and literary activity, and finally, of his character.

I INTELLECTUAL DEVELOPMENT

1. *Formative Philosophical Influence*—It is a matter of interest both to inquire the nature of the intellectual equipment with which Beneke began his renewed career at Berlin and to indicate the lines of his philosophical development. The early writings of Beneke themselves bear ample testimony to the formative influences at work upon the promising young philosopher; but, if it were needed, we have the personal testimony of Beneke himself. In later years some German critics, especially Drobisch,[1] savagely attacked the character of Beneke, claiming that he was little more than a Herbartian pure and simple; that he had sought to give the appearance of originality to his system more through new terms than new ideas; and that he had given himself a good deal of uncalled-for trouble in trying to differentiate himself from Herbart. Beneke, in a valuable comparison of his own psychology with that of Herbart,[2] took occasion in a histor-

---

[1] See *Die Neue Psychologie*, pp. 76–77.
[2] Ibid. Dritter Aufsatz: "*Ueber das Verhältniss meiner Psychologie zur Herbart'schen*," pp. 76–144.

ical preliminary to answer the unfounded charge against both his character and his system.

So far as the influence of Herbart on Beneke is concerned, to see its lack one has only to recall the inherent character of his earliest three writings, to the fundamental principles of which Beneke, as he himself claimed, remained true throughout his whole career. These principles were indeed so opposed in method to that of Herbart that the "empiricism" of Beneke was in his early days the very ground of his being regarded a resolute opponent both of Herbart and of the speculative or metaphysical method for which he stood. It is true that Beneke later read with grateful appreciation Herbart's works, with some conclusions of which his own results in part coincided. But the germs of his developed system were already almost all clearly indicated in the works mentioned, and at the time of writing these Beneke knew little or nothing of Herbart's philosophy. On this point Beneke has left an interesting record. He says: "In the time of my real mental formation, in the time when my previously thoroughly fleeting and changing spirit began to assume a definitely fixed form and build up the fundamental tendencies which it afterwards for the most part followed throughout my whole life almost unchanged, Herbart was entirely unknown to me. I had made, in addition to the admirable English philosophers, German philosophical investigators, particularly Kant, Jacobi, Fries (at the suggestion of De Wette), Platner and Garve, the object of laborious study. The influence of all these, in my first three writings, in the 'Theory of Knowledge,' 'Empirical Psychology,' and 'Doctor's Dissertation,' is not to be mistaken; of any influence of Herbart not a trace is found. * * * Of course there are to be found already in these incomplete youthful essays various traces of what the direction of my psychological investigations made common to me and to

Herbart, *e. g.*, of the polemic against innate abstract psychical powers. But how differently is this grounded, and how differently carried out! Compare especially pages 54–73 of the 'Empirical Psychology.' The rejection of the previous theory and the definition of what is to be put in the place of it was accomplished *inductively*, on the basis of a comparison of the products of *inner observation*, without the slightest intermixture of speculative foundations."[3]

The more positive influences on his early development Beneke has set forth in the passage just quoted. Perhaps a word further deserves to be said of the influence of English thought upon him. He had a complete mastery of the English tongue; corresponded in English with many English philosophers and educationalists, among them Sir William Hamilton and Dr. Arnold of Rugby; and his works are a lasting monument to his extended scholarship not only in English philosophy[4] but in English literature as well. To mention all the philosophical works with which he showed personal acquaintance would be to enumerate about all the English philosophers from Bacon and Locke down to John Stuart Mill. His writings show that he was perhaps more directly influenced by Locke and Hume, and by the contemporary Scottish philosophers, in whose works, especially those of Brown and Stewart, he took a keen critical interest.

2. *Relation to Kant*—(a) The connecting clue to the

---

[3] *Die Neue Psychologie*, pp. 80–81. On this point compare also Ueberweg, Vol. II, p. 282.—"Not until his first three works (Outlines of the Science of Cognition, Empirical Psychology as the Basis of all Knowledge, and *De veris philosophiæ initiis*, his Doctor's Dissertation) had already appeared (in 1820) did he become acquainted with one of Herbart's works; that work was the second edition of the Introduction to Philosophy (1821); until then he had possessed only a superficial knowledge (acquired perhaps through Stiedenroth's *Theorie des Wissens*, Göttingen, 1819,) of Herbart's views."

[4] See an interesting sketch by Beneke of the contemporary philosophical standpoint in England in *Die Neue Psychologie*, pp. 300–336.

philosophical development of Beneke during the days of his activity at Berlin is the philosophy of Kant. Of this system Beneke from the outset showed himself a keen critic. And in no point keener than in his discussions of the "internal sense" and of the employment of the *a priori* method. His attitude towards Kant in these respects, however, will be considered with more detail in the subsequent exposition of his philosophy.

(b) There is one point, however, in respect to Beneke's relation to Kant, that calls for special emphasis. The historical importance of Beneke as the real pioneer of "the movement back to Kant," has never been sufficiently recognized, or more than that, it has not been recognized at all.[5] While Beneke, single handed, spent much of his effort in refuting Kant, and especially the *a priori* method as it was afterwards developed in the philosophies of Fichte, Schelling and Hegel, nevertheless, for him, in the Kantian system was to be found the true foundation and starting point for philos-

---

[5] Falckenberg, in his History, p. 589, speaking of the more modern "movement back to Kant," says: "The Kantian philosophy has created two epochs: one at the time of its appearance, and the second two generations after the death of its author. The new Kantian movement, which is one of the most prominent characteristics of the philosophy of the present time, took its beginnings a quarter of a century ago. It is true that even before 1865 individual thinkers like Ernst Reinhold of Jena (died 1855), the admirer of Fries, J. B. Meyer, of Bonn, K. G. von Reichlin-Meldegg, and others, had sought a point of departure for their views in Kant; that K. Fischer's work on Kant, 1860, had given a lively impulse to the renewed study of the critical philosophy; nay, that the cry, "Back to Kant," had been expressly raised by Fortlage (as early as 1832, in his treatise, The Gaps in the Hegelian System), and by Zeller."

Falckenberg thus, while tracing the movement even so far back as to Fortlage, ignores Beneke. But the real "opening gun" of this movement was Beneke's little Kantian Memorial, in celebration of the fiftieth anniversary of the *Critique of Pure Reason*. While the imprint of the book is 1832, as the prefatory note shows, it had been written and finished before November, 1831. Fortlage, moreover, who had been one of Beneke's students, and was an ardent admirer of him and his system, doubtless had imbibed many of his views on this point.

ophy. In a little book,[6] which has deserved a better fate at the hands of historians of German philosophy, and which is perhaps destined to become of permanent historical value[7] for its picture of the philosophical situation of the times, he expressly advocates the need of a return to a criticised Kantian basis, and indeed towards this end much of his life's activity was directed. Beneke's express statement is contained in the closing paragraph of the introduction, in which he pictures the condition of a philosophical Germany become, in the terms of Sir James Mackintosh, "metaphysically mad." He says: "It is also high time that we became conscious of the confusion which for so long a time now has prevailed with the highest and most venerated among us, under the pretext of representing the inner being of all things in their purest truth. If we do not wish to expose ourselves to the danger of having the sore, which has been healed on the one side, break out again on the other in only more perilous form, *we must direct our criticism* not to the daughter and granddaughter philosophies, but *to the Kantian philosophy itself*, in order where possible to lay bare the very root of the evil in this, and to stop at the source the stream which threatens to inundate Germany with an intellectual barbarism."[8]

[6] *Kant und die philosophische Aufgabe unserer Zeit. Eine Jubeldenkschrift auf die Kritik der reinen Vernunft.* Berlin, 1832.

[7] An interesting confirmation of the judgment here expressed is to be found in Bergmann's *Geschichte der Philosophie* (Berlin, 1893). Bergmann in his article on Beneke has palpably and expressly made valuable use of the Kant Memorial. It may be scarcely necessary to repeat (see Introductory Note) that the present work was planned and completely written entirely without any knowledge of Bergmann's History, which only fell into the writer's hands as the work is going to press.

[8] *Kant und die philosophische Aufgabe*, p. 11.

II LIFE EFFORT AND LITERARY ACTIVITY

1. *Opposition to the Philosophical Tendencies of the Times*—Beneke's little memorial on "Kant and the Philosophical Problem of our Time," has a peculiar significance, because it is indicative of what was really his life effort—a profound critical opposition to the philosophical tendencies of the times. This opposition was not one directed against either an individual or individuals; it was an earnest and serious effort to bring back the German mind to the narrow path of truth, from which in Beneke's view it was sadly erring. In pursuance of this object, Beneke had issued the book above mentioned, the second but most important work issued by him after his return to Berlin. In this book, which was intended as a commemoration of the semi-centennial of Kant's *Critique of Pure Reason*, first issued in 1781, he set forth in no uncertain terms his attitude towards the prevailing tendencies. The purpose of the Kantian Memorial was threefold: 1. To examine the fundamental tendencies of the Kantian *Critique*, and discover the inherent reasons for its failure to accomplish its avowed purpose; 2. To show in general outline the character of the later German systems as conditioned on the Kantian point of view; 3. To glance at the future outlook.

Beneke is very severe in his denunciation of the purely metaphysical character of the later German systems. He says: "When Fichte regards the Ego as going out of itself in an unending activity, as setting before it a barrier or the Non-ego, and returning from this to itself, what else have we here but a metaphor?—for in no proper sense can we possibly assign to an entirely non-spatial spirit such movements in space. When later the Schellingian school talk of the poles of the absolute, of the disuniting of these, of a decaying of ideas; or Hegel speaks of the going forth from itself of the abstract to its non-being, and of a return of the same into itself; these are all symbols which it can enter into the minds of no one to apply as truly scientific predicates, from the construction of which a true conception of scientific knowledge can be gained." [9]

Beneke too is very summary in his rejection of the view, then very prevalent, that German philosophy was to be regarded as a systematic development ending with Hegel. The claims of the later systems to a Kantian foundation were regarded by him as utterly false. "We have, it is asserted," he says, "not merely philosophical systems, such as no other people have, but also a *systematic evolution of philosophy itself* from Kant to Schelling and Hegel; and so perhaps must the same fundamental ideas return ever in new form. A fine repetition of our systems is the systematic development of our philosophy! Does it call itself the follower of Kant? Does it assert that it is his spirit that suggests its speculation to it? Nothing could be more desirable than that people should once for all give a clear account of precisely what they understand by this. Kant taught on every page that only on the foundations of *experience* could true knowledge, knowledge of reality, be acquired; whereas it pushes the knowledge gained through experience contemptuously into the background, in order to possess a far higher kind of knowledge in the pure imagination, and in its chimerical process of construction. Kant is ever coming back to this point, that out of mere *concepts* no knowledge of the existing is possible, that all speculative reasoning leads only to chimeras, that the suprasensible can never for us men become the object of *intuition* or of *contemplation*, can never be *known* by us, but only comprehended through moral *faith;* whereas this derides *faith* in the suprasensible as a minor accomplishment belonging to the spirit; and their whole philosophy is from beginning to end a *theory* of

---

[9] *Kant und die Philosophische Aufgabe*, pp. 41-42.

the suprasensible, which it asserts itself to be able to know in its *inner being;* and therefore it employs itself also with speculation, which Kant, as being unattainable for all time to the human spirit, wished to have banished from all philosophy. Kant, although he was called back by them, made, as did Socrates and his school, *morality* the central point of all philosophy; whereas it has so placed morality in the shade that people have rightly doubted whether perhaps it could be introduced in the construction of their phisolophical systems, except as a most unpardonable inconsistency. Such a system then is *in the fullest opposition* to Kant."[10]

Almost before the ink was dry on the manuscript pages of the book just quoted, Hegel died. This was on November 14, 1831. Beneke was a man of too much character to incur even the suspicion that his book had been immediately written as a vindictive stab at the dead Hegel. Undoubtedly, therefore, it is Hegel's death to which he refers in the following short prefatory note to the volume: "In order to avoid all misinterpretation, I may remark that the present volume by no means first originated in consequence of recent events, but already in August of this year was ready for publication, but this was prevented at that time by the outbreak of cholera in our state. As for the rest, the book speaks for itself."[11]

Lectures and Writings—It certainly is significant of the chief source of opposition to Beneke that in a very short time after Hegel's death, *i. e.*, in 1832, he was appointed a professor *extraordinarius* (although not till nine years after did he receive any salary).[12] While the keen edge of the oppo-

---

[10] Ibid, pp. 83–84. [11] Ibid. *Vorerinnerung.*

[12] Compare the remarks of Dr. Schmidt, *Pädagogisches Jahrbuch*, 1856, p. 15. So lasting, however, was the Hegelian opposition, that a petition to make Beneke a regular professor, signed by over 800 members of a schoolmasters' convention, held in Dresden in 1848, and some 200 others, gotten up unknown to Beneke by Dressler, and sent by him to Minister Rodbertus at Berlin, proved, notwithstanding Beneke's twenty-one years of continuous and unremitting service, unsuccessful. Cf. Dressler's article, *Pädagogisches Jahrbuch*, pp. 31–32.

sition to him was thus removed, nevertheless throughout the rest of his career he was overshadowed by the accredited Hegelian system, and there is something almost pathetic in the way in which, in his lectures and writings, he endeavored, single-handed and alone, to stem the overwhelming current of the prevailing philosophical speculation.

Dressler has left an interesting note regarding Beneke's lectures, which, on his first personal acquaintance with Beneke in 1841, he attended. "He had very attentive hearers," he says, "but their number was small; in the year 1841, and following, only what proceeded from Hegel had any influence, and he often had to undergo the experience of having advanced students leave him, after one lecture to which they had listened, with the remark: 'That indeed is nothing more than sound common sense.' Since the students knew on whom they would be examined, on whom not, who had influence for their promotion, and who not, whose philosophy was thought proper high up, whose was put down with a black mark, they did what accorded with their worldly interest, and the teacher whom they much more willingly would have listened to they left almost deserted. When it is known what a wretched delivery many professors had whose lecture rooms nevertheless were always filled, Beneke seems like a true martyr."[13]

Beneke's writings are by no means merely destructive criticism. They offer in the place of that which they attempt to destroy positive constructive work. I shall not attempt to enumerate here all of even the important works which Beneke put forth during this period. He had the usual voluminousness of all the German philosophical writers, and there is a certain profusion and repetition about a good deal of his writing, due to the fact that his whole system centered about his fundamental psychological principles, which thus

---

[13] Dressler, *Pädagogisches Jahrbuch*, 1856, pp. 25-26.

in each work receive new statement and application. The central work of all Beneke's writings is the *Lehrbuch der Psychologie als Naturwissenschaft*, first published in 1833. The permanent value of this book may be inferred from the fact that it has reached four editions,[14] two after the death of Beneke. It is the central work, because, as Dressler says, " it presents with the greatest precision the principles of the new psychology," and because, we may add, the new psychology was the fundamental basis of Beneke's whole system. *Die neue Psychologie (Erlaüternde Aufsätze zur Zweiten Auflage meines Lehrbuchs der Psychologie als Naturwissenschaft*, Berlin, 1845), is important for its further elucidation of Beneke's psychological principles, and also for the comparison with Herbart, already alluded to.

Beneke's metaphysical standpoint is to be found in part in almost all his writings, but his complete views are gathered together in the *System der Metaphysik und der Religions Philosophie, aus den natürlichen Grundverhältnissen des menschlichen Geistes abgeleitet*, Berlin, 1840.

The most important applications of his system are to be found in his *Erziehungs und Unterrichtslehre*, two volumes, the third edition of which was edited by Dressler in 1864; and in the " *Grundlinien des natürlichen Systemes der praktischen Philosophie.*" The latter consisted of three volumes: I. General Ethics; II. Special Ethics; III. The Outlines of Natural Law, of Politics, and of the Philosophy of Criminal Law. Dressler says Beneke regarded his Ethics as his most successful work. One other most influential application of his system was the " *System der Logik als Kunstlehre des Denkens*," Berlin, 1842. This was on the basis of the *Lehrbuch der Logik*, which Beneke issued in 1832, and in which he had already anticipated by a number

---

[14] Second edition, 1845; 3d ed., 1861; 4th ed., Berlin, 1877, edited and with an appendix characterizing Beneke's whole works, by Johann Gottlieb Dressler.

of years the new logical theories over the discovery of which Sir William Hamilton and de Morgan got into controversy.[15]

III CHARACTER

Throughout the whole trying period of his life activity at Berlin, the character of Beneke stands out in shining relief. Pure and manly in his life, loving and affectionate among his intimates, faithful and strong in his friendships, forbearing towards his enemies, zealous for the truth, he won the love and admiration of all who came in close contact with him.

It is interesting to compare the loving tributes of his friends on these points. Diesterweg in his tribute says: "As a man he was what the ancients called an *anima candida* (a pure soul); I believe that he went forth from this world as unspotted as a pure girl."[16] Schmidt says: "That he felt and lived in the spirit of Christianity, he showed in the fact that he forgave his enemies, defended his antagonists, and where necessity demanded, hastened to bring consolation and assistance."[17] Dittes, in a letter to Dressler,[18] speaks of his "frank rejection of what was untenable; his friendly recognition of success; his earnestness in the apprehension of life, and his affectionate interest in my whole being, inner and outer." Fortlage, in the course of a long and glowing tribute, says:

"There still rings in my ears the sound of the melodious and gentle voice with which he always in his lectures, without passion or violence, answered even the most irritating invectives against his assertions. The ability to attach himself to others, or to form a coterie about him, was as foreign and unintelligible to him as personal enmity. Moreover, he knew very well his separate and forlorn position among the scientific factions, but he stuck by it with the most tenacious,

---

[15] See Dressler's *Kurze Charaktertstik*, appended to the fourth edition of Beneke's *Lehrbuch der Psychologie*, p. 299.

[16] *Pädagogisches Jahrbuch*, 1856, p. 1.   [17] Ibid., p. 19.   [18] Ibid., p. 23.

yet mildest pertinacity, so that in very truth he broke his path through no other means than those of his own single self. * * * Slight and public neglect, which usually in others has aroused rage and resentment, died away in his harmonious soul with a feeling of sorrow for the blind fascination with which his age still shut itself up entirely from a knowledge, in the perfecting of which mankind still has to await the most preferable remedy for its wounds and infirmities. But although no feeling of wrath ever secured a place in his soul, still any yielding to fate or placability towards the ruling intellectual tendencies was just as little known to it."[19]

To sum it up in the words of Dressler: "One of the most prominent traits of his noble character was his great forbearance towards his often malicious opponents, to whom he occasioned more disquiet than perhaps was exactly agreeable, and I could furnish several authentic proofs on this point if higher considerations did not preclude this. Not that he did not feel deeply the injustice done him, but his lofty spirit, his pure soul, soon raised him again above the pain and taught him to laugh at the apparent triumph of the world."[20]

Beneke met his death in a mysterious way. On March 1, 1854, he suddenly disappeared. His brother (with whom, since he never married, he lived in Berlin), Diesterweg, and other friends, made most protracted searches for him, but to no avail. He had suffered much in recent years from *insomnia*, and it was finally believed that he had wandered off and taken his own life. Not until June, 1856, was his body recovered. It was then found in the canal near Charlottenburg by some workmen. The exact time and manner of his death ever remained a mystery.

[19] Fortlage, *Acht Psychologische Vorträge: Fierter Vortrag*, "*Ueber den Charakter*," Jena, 1872, pp. 170–172.

[20] *Pädagogisches Jahrbuch*, 1856, p. 32.

PART II

THE PHILOSOPHY

CHAPTER I

HISTORICAL BASIS AND THEORY OF KNOWLEDGE

§ 1. *General Introduction*—The exposition of Beneke's philosophical system which follows, being intended rather as an introduction to the further study of Beneke, concerns itself more particularly with the foundation principles. These principles, as has already been pointed out, are to be found in completest statement in the *Lehrbuch der Psychologie*, which, therefore, is made the basis of the text. Where, however, for the fuller elucidation of various parts of the system, it has seemed necessary, further reference has been made to Beneke's other works, duly indicated in the foot-notes. A comparison of the text following with that of the *Lehrbuch* will show that while Beneke's form of statement in many particular paragraphs has been closely followed, the general method of exposition has been radically different. The *Lehrbuch*, being practically a compendium of the whole system, necessarily fails, by its dogmatic deductive method, to preserve the inherent coerciveness of the fundamental theory. The attempt, therefore, has been made, by a more inductive statement, to minimize the apparent arbitrariness of some of the fundamental conclusions. It is hoped that this plan may thus help to reveal something of the true significance of Beneke's thinking in the development of German idealism.

Among the Germans, Beneke's significance has been largely psychological, but psychological in the sense of immediate applicability to pedagogics. His chief following, therefore, has been among the school-masters of Germany, and the superior value of his psychology, in its pedagogical, logical and ethical applications, has made this psychology not only a formidable rival of, but in high educational circles, preferable to the Herbartian.[1] For while possessing all the distinct psychological merits usually attributed to the Herbartian system, Beneke's psychology enjoys the additional merit of an even profounder metaphysical basis, reached by a more satisfactory and tenable method. And indeed, since Beneke's real importance in this respect has never been recognized either in Germany or elsewhere, it is the metaphysical significance of his system that the following pages distinctly aim to bring out.

In pursuance of the aim and plan indicated, the present chapter takes up the consideration of the historical basis of the system with the view of setting in a clear light its starting point.

[1] Diesterweg, who especially in his *Pädagogisches Jahrbuch*, has exerted a powerful influence in the education of German teachers, and who for years was a leader of educational affairs in Berlin, was an ardent admirer and advocate of Beneke's system. In the course of his tribute to Beneke, in the *Jahrbuch für 1856* (p. 4), Diesterweg sums up the essence of German pedagogy in a sentence which deserves to be preseved, because it is the keynote of all pedagogics: "*Who would educate and mould the human soul, must know it; who would educate and mould individuals, must possess the power to comprehend their individuality.*" I quote this to give force to the statement which almost immediately follows. After expressing the conviction that without rational psychology there can be no scientific pedagogics, he adds: "Inasmuch as in our estimation the Benekian psychology does more in these respects than any other, until that 'other' appears, we shall hold fast to it, and recommend it for study to the teachers who feel the need of acting with a clear consciousness of what they are doing."

I DOCTRINES OF PERCEPTION BEFORE KANT

§ 2. *Shortcomings of Earlier Doctrines of Perception*—Notwithstanding the shortcomings of the doctrine of perception up to the time of Kant, from all this early analysis there comes a clear gain which shows itself in the recognition of all individual experience as a form of consciousness, and in the sharp distinction of this experience into two strikingly contrasted aspects—" external" consciousness and " internal" consciousness. This distinction Hume attempted to indicate by the terms " impressions" and " ideas"; Berkeley had recognized it in the terms " ideas of sensation" (also " real things") and " ideas proper"; thus both Berkeley and Hume, although recognizing the conscious character of both impressions and ideas, attempted to rescue the word " idea" from the reprehensible use to which Locke had put it by making it do service for both things and thought. But valuable as these distinctions undoubtedly are, they fall far short of a complete accounting for experience. The full import of the philosophical question which experience presses on us for solution, seems never to have completely dawned on the earlier English philosophers. Locke, it is true, recognized, although only in a descriptive way, the synthetic function or activity of mind in originating complex ideas, but he failed to see that a like activity was implied also in the so-called simple ideas or sensations; as a result he never gets beyond the natural history of some particular idea to the fundamental question how an idea is at all possible. Berkeley, too, utterly failed to grasp the problem involved in perception. For him, " things," while existing in the mental realm of the given perceiving individual, were " mere aggregations of sensations." " Thus, for example," he says,[2] " a certain color, taste, smell, figure and consistence having been observed to

[2] *Principles of Human Knowledge*, p. 36 (Fraser's *Selections from Berkeley*, Oxford, 1884).

go together, are accounted one distinct thing, signified by the name of *apple;* other collections of ideas constitute a stone, a tree, a book, and the like sensible things. But, as Professor Fraser, in commenting on the passage quoted, acutely remarks:[3] "Is *mere* 'observation' enough to account for this synthesis, in which *ideas* or *phenomena* are aggregated, and thus converted into *things?*" How such "collections of ideas" could take place at all without some such synthesis, is by Berkeley entirely overlooked. It is in Hume that this oversight becomes completest. For to Hume, both the groupings of conscious states called "things" or impressions, as well as the ideas which were supposed to be faint copies of the original impressions, did not possess even that small degree of unity or coherence which Berkeley at least implied for them by assigning them an existence within a spiritual substance or soul. Individual experience, so far as it could be called individual, was to Hume " but a bundle or collection of different perceptions which succeed each other with inconceivable rapidity, and are in a perpetual flux and movement."[4] With this conception of experience as a mosaic of co-existent but fleeting *discrete* feelings, Hume brought the whole problem of perception to the sharpest issue. And it was the needed solution to this problem that Kant attempted to supply.

II THE KANTIAN THEORY

§ 3. *General Character of the Problem as Presented to Kant* —While the general character of the philosophical problem as it presented itself to the mind of Kant was thus already predetermined for him by English thinkers, it was also largely determined by the preceding metaphysical speculation on the continent. The Scylla and Charybdis through which Kant had to steer his philosophic course was really

[3] Ibid., p. 36, note.
[4] *Treatise of Human Nature*, p. 252 (Ed. Selby-Bigge, Oxford, 1888).

on the one hand the skepticism of Hume, on the other, the rationalism of Wolf.

As against Hume, the doctrine of Kant confirms all experience as a form of consciousness or knowledge in a sense which shows the utter inadequacy of the psychological atomism of Hume to do service even as a description of experience such as we know it. Outer experience, on the one hand, it demonstrates is utterly unintelligible and even impossible as a "mere aggregate" of sensations. Unrelated feelings could never constitute or alone yield knowledge. Only so far as the manifold of sense is apprehended as a unit does experience in the sense of a perceptive consciousness become possible. Inner experience, on the other hand, is shown to be likewise impossible as a mere collection of ideas or abstractions from the perceptive consciousness. The essential characteristic of inner experience is that it too is the apprehension of the many as one, and this is only to say that the essential condition of the existence of every idea is the unifying activity necessarily implied in it.

As against Wolf, the doctrine of Kant insisted on the impossibility of reason, through mere explication of its alleged innate ideas, ever reaching metaphysical truth. Inner experience, or the conceptive consciousness, since the days of Descartes, had been elevated to the position not merely of sole philosophical criterion, but of a criterion valid apart from all experience, so far as that word refers to external perceptions. Clearness of conception was for the Cartesians the test of truth, so that within the idea itself was implicitly contained the whole measure and content of truth. This doctrine and its concomitant one of innate ideas reached its climax in Wolf, who, for example, in his Logic (c. 1, § 6,) says:[5] "Whether our notions of external things are conveyed

---

[5] Quoted by St. John. See his edition of Locke's *Essay Concerning Human Understanding*, p. 140, note. (*Works of John Locke*, London, 1889).

into the soul as into an empty receptacle, or whether rather they be not buried, as it were, in the essence of the soul, and are brought forth barely by his own powers, on occasion of the changes produced in our bodies by external objects, is a question at present foreign to this place. In my 'Thoughts on God and the Human Soul,' chap. v., I shall there only be able to show that the last opinion is the more agreeable to truth."

Thus, then, as against the attempt of Hume to interpret experience as an empirical chaos of sense impressions, so against this effort of the traditional philosophy to evolve knowledge of reality from mere inner consciousness, Kant was obliged to revolt.

§ 4. *Aim of the Kantian Philosophy*—The fundamental aim, therefore, of the Kantian philosophy, as Beneke points out,[6] was first a purely negative one. Its chief effort was spent in " thoroughly grounding and establishing this proposition: that *through mere concepts no knowledge of an existing thing* is possible, nor is there possible any proof of the existence of the thing thought in this concept." Thus as against the traditional philosophy, which out of mere concepts believed itself able to demonstrate the existence of its objects, and the inner nature of things, the existence of God, etc., Kant urged the distinction between knowledge and mere thinking. "For mere thinking we have enough in our concept, but in this we acquire nothing but mere thought-forms, in order out of the given intuitions to make knowledge. *Knowledge, on the contrary, in so far as it asserts an existence*, is given only through the perception (*Wahrnehmung*) of that which exists."[7] Or to put Kant's opposition between the Understanding and Sense in his own words: "*Der*

---

[6] *Kant und die philosophische Aufgabe unserer Zeit*, p. 12.
[7] Ibid, p. 13.

Verstand vermag nichts anzuschauen, und die Sinne nichts zudenken. Nur daraus, das sie sich vereinigen, kann Erkenntniss entspringen." [8] Or again: "Without sensibility no object would be given to us, without understanding none would be thought. Thoughts without content are empty, perceptions without conceptions are blind." [9]

But this negative result, Beneke further points out, was reached by Kant only to pave the way for "two highly important positive aims." First, to bring the ruling mental power, which by its method had lost itself in the unraveling of an insoluble metaphysical problem, back to experience, and thereby concentrate its energy on empirical knowledge (*Erfahrungs-erkenntniss*), which promises a richer and quicker progress. Second, "Kant wished 'to get rid of knowledge in order to make room for faith.' Since for us on knowledge of supra-sensible is possible, the belief in God, Immortality, and Freedom possesses certainty for us only as postulates of the Practical Reason." [10]

§ 5. *The Kantian Theory of Knowledge as stated by Beneke* —Beneke thus had a clear conception of the aim of the Kantian philosophy, and he states its theory of knowledge thus:—"According to Kant's oft repeated statements we must look upon all human knowledge as a product: as a product, on the one side, of the material of knowledge, or of sensuous impressions furnished by the object; on the other, of the forms arising from the knowing subject, which forms again are twofold,—the pure forms of intuition of space and time, and the pure forms of the understanding, or categories. It is in virtue of the first named factors that our knowledge finds its truly objective foundation: for through sense impressions is something supplied to it from the object; but

---

[8] Quoted by Beneke, ibid., p. 13.
[9] Watson's *Selections from Kant*, p. 41 (Glasgow, 1888).
[10] *Kant und die philosophische Aufgabe*, p. 17.

still we do not apprehend the objects as they are in and for themselves independent of our perceptions of them, but only in relation to our faculty of knowledge, or (in other words) as they *appear* to us (*i. e.* as phenomena). To phenomena we are limited in all our knowledge: for indeed we are in no manner able to resolve this product into its simple factors; and the object in itself consequently remains for us necesrarily a thing absolutely unknown, and of which we can only surmise, not assert anything absolutely. According to Kant's oft repeated explanations, this holds just as true of the existence of our own soul, as of the existence of outer being. * * * * Even ourselves consequently we know only as phenomena; and the being of our own soul, how it exists in and for itself and independent of this way of knowing it, for us remains forever entirely unknown."

§ 6. *The Kantian Distinction of Knowledge Independent of Experience*—To understand Beneke's criticism of the theory of knowledge just stated, it is necessary first to get clear Kant's pseudo-distinction of knowledge independent of experience. With the English introspectionists Kant recognized all experience as a mode of knowledge implying intelligence. But he differed from Locke, Berkeley and Hume, in seeing that this intelligence " has a rule of its own, which must be an *a priori* condition of all knowledge of objects presented to it."[12] The perceptive consciousness, then, is not, as Locke and Berkeley maintained, mere groupings of simple sensations or collections of ideas; nor as Hume, a mere chaos of disconnected separate sense phenomena; it is an indeterminate manifold which has been brought under the unity of certain determinate relations. " Perception," says Kant, " can become knowledge only if it is related in some way to the object which it determines." Perception, then, is

[11] Ibid., pp. 26–27.
[12] Watson's *Selections from Kant*, p. 4.

really the determination of an object, and this determination becomes effected through conceptions. Only then in so far as objects, not actually present to consciousness (whatever we may mean by such so-called "objects"), "conform to the constitution of our faculty of perception,"[13] can they enter the conscious plane or become knowledge for us. Objects of experience, then, and by these Kant seems to mean objects within the perceptive consciousness (objects of outer experience), are to be taken in two distinct senses,—"on the one hand, as a phenomenon, and on the other hand, as a thing in itself." Criticism establishes our unavoidable ignorance of things in themselves, and limits all we can *know* to mere phenomena.

But since experience, inner or outer, is a form of consciousness, and so of knowledge, and since knowledge, it is alleged, is a *product* of two factors, it is surprising to find Kant, on the basis so far outlined, raising in the *Critique of Pure Reason* the question, "as a question which cannot be lightly put aside," "whether there is any knowledge that is independent of experience, and even of all impressions of sense."[14] If experience, consciousness, is made up of two elements, sense material and mental form, what can it mean to inquire concerning knowledge "*absolutely* independent of all experience?" It must mean either of two things: 1st. Is there any knowledge that is not a product of two factors? or, 2nd. Is there any knowledge of which one of the factors is not *sense* material? To emphasize this point is to bring into clear light a most important confusion which results from Kant's juggle with the word "experience." The word experience, so far as that word is intended to mean knowledge of the existence of an object, is limited again and again by Kant to the perceptive consciousness (outer experience). The conceptive or purely subjective consciousness (inner

---

[13] Ibid., p. 3.   [14] Ibid., p. 8.

experience) is recognized by him only far enough to show its impotency to yield knowledge of the existence of things in themselves (*Dingen-an-sich*), or of the thing thought (*Noumenon*). But without deciding at the moment, whether in external sense perception we get at the existence of the thing known, whereas (as Kant contends), in internal sense perception, we do not, this much at least we may insist on, that, regardless of the *content* or meaning—regardless of the existence or non-existence of *that to which they refer*—the facts of inner experience (memories, imaginations, concepts), as *psychical existences*, are just as much parts of or data of the individual experience as any of the sense perceptions of outer experience.

§7. *Beneke's Criticism of the Kantian Theory of Knowledge*—It is the recognition of this confusion in Kant's use of the word experience, in the sense of knowledge of existence, that constitutes the basis of Beneke's criticism of his theory. Beneke insists on the inherent contradiction of Kant's general position. This contradiction lay on the one hand in regarding knowledge, perceptive and conceptive, as phenomenalistic, and yet pretending to a knowledge of the factors by which it was produced. If knowledge is to be regarded as mere appearance, as a product of two factors, the sense material and the forms of the understanding, then for the strictly logical Kantian, the latter must remain as unknowable as the former. Or, as Beneke puts it: "The pure intuitions of space and time are on the part of the subject to form the simple basal elements of our phenomenalistic knowledge. It is impossible moreover that they can themselves become again appearances. Knowledge of appearances, as product, has for factors, on one side, the sense impressions of the object, on the other, the knowledge forms of our soul; and just as the objective cause, or that through which feeling is effected, is a thing-in-itself, so beyond doubt must also the pure forms of intuition and the pure concepts of the understanding which form the subjective cause, be things-in-themselves. How too, would it be possible to acquire a knowledge of these subjective causes through experience, since experience in truth, according to the Kantian system, permits nothing to be known but appearances, and so is as little able to bring at all within its reach things-in-themselves, not merely in respect of our own soul's existence but in respect of the outer world as well?"[15]

Beneke rejects a suggestion, which he himself makes, that the basal forms of human knowlehge might have been introduced by Kant as *hypotheses*, for the acceptance of which we must make further comparison with experience, "just as in the natural sciences we introduce the force of gravitation, the force of electricity, and in general all forces, which indeed no one has power to see or otherwise experience *as forces*, but which we, in order to gain some coherency among our experiences, first hypothetically assume, and then corroborate through comparison of consequences deduced from them with genuinely given experiences."[16] But Beneke's reason for not accepting this suggestion, not to mention Kant's express rejection of hypothesis in critical philosophy, is that inasmuch as experience, according to Kant's own principles, could never at all attain to the in-itselfness of the thing (*An-sich der Dinge*), it never could reach it even intermediately, and so could not corroborate it at all.

The fundamental error then of the Kantian system, to Beneke's mind, lay in regarding, on the one side, the objective in-itselfness, the x of the thing, on the other, the subjective forms, which also are things in themselves, as working together for the production of knowledge. In so doing Kant was already surreptitiously applying the causal relation

---

[15] *Kant und die philosophische Aufgabe*, pp. 28–29. [16] Ibid., p. 31.

to things-in-themselves, "which Kant in the most exact language," says Beneke, "shows as utterly inadmissible." Thus then the Kantian theory contained within itself an irresolvable contradiction. While pretending to know those powers and forms of the mind which constituted the very conditions of experience, according to its own fundamental view, these powers and forms were in no manner knowable; neither immediately through experience, since this is limited to product or appearance, and so cannot reach either unity or in-itselfness; nor independent of experience (i. e. through the conceptive consciousness), for of the existence of what is constructed in this way out of mere concepts we have no assurance.

§ 8. *Beneke's Resolution of the Inherent Contradiction of the Kantian Theory*—Beneke attempts to resolve the fundamental contradiction inherent in the system of Kant first by the restoration of "inner experience" to at least a parity with "outer experience." The word experience he insists must be made to include *inner* as well as outer experience. The facts of inner experience, memories, imaginations, concepts, etc., are as truly realities for any given individual as the sense perceptions of his outer experience. The *object* of any given idea, the *content* of some particular concept, may indeed be, in one case, e. g., the analytic unity which the understanding gives to concepts, or in another, the synthetic unity which it gives to percepts. This unity, this "form of the understanding," may be indeed *in itself* unknown; so far as it is what is *meant*, or what is *known* by the particular concept, it only *appears*. But the given concept, apart from its content, is still to be recognized as a *psychical existence;* it is still, in the passing, as much a reality in the conscious experience of an individual as any given perception. And, moreover, it is in virtue of the nature of its content that we classify it as a fact of inner experience rather than of outer.

Therefore, even though we regard for the moment the facts of inner experience also as mere appearances, it is a great gain if we clearly recognize that both aspects of experience, inner and outer, are forms of consciousness, or knowledge, and in this respect at least are on an equal plane.

§ 9. *Internal Sense Yields Knowledge of a Thing in itself*[17]—But while both forms of conscious experience, outer and inner, *as existences*, or as having *being*, are to be regarded on an equal plane,—in their phenomenal aspect, that is, in respect to the knowledge which they yield, these two forms, Beneke claims, are essentially different. In inner experience, in "inner sense," we have no mere knowledge of phenomena, but of a thing as it is in and for itself. The claim of the new idealism, he says,[18] "that our perceptions of our own psychical existence have not the least superiority over our perceptions of the outer world, since, in the former case as well as the latter, it is impossible to compare the perceived being with our perception of it, has on closer observation no other ground than a false parallel between the outer sense and the so-called inner sense: which now, because it too is called "sense," must, it is supposed, stand in like relations to the perceived thing as the former. The thing perceived through outer sense we cannot of course (in accordance with our previously gained conviction) apprehend in its complete truth, because we are not able *to go out of ourselves to the thing*. But this reason indeed falls to the ground in respect to the perception of our own selves: *we have the presented psychical existence immediately in our power*, inasmuch as we, the perceiving existence, are at the same time also that which is perceived; and consequently, since that which is perceived is just as near and as inner as that which does the perceiving, there is no

---

[17] Compare further §§ 97 and 98.
[18] *Das Verhältniss von Seele und Leib*, (Göttingen, 1826), p. 43.

need of demanding of us the impossible feat of going out of ourselves to become another."

§ 10. *Permanent Value of the Kantian Analysis*—The permanent gain resulting from the Kantian analysis, thought Beneke, is the clear recognition of knowledge, perceptive and conceptive, as a *process* as well as product, and the irresistible emphasis which in spite of itself it lays upon *inner experience*. The first wide opposition between the Kantian and other theories of knowledge was that the former regarded empirical psychology as entirely useless for furnishing it with a foundation. Empirical psychology, according to it, had value only as applied philosophy, to which pure philosophy handed over its principles *a priori*. In spite of his fundamental contention that conception can yield no knowledge of existence, and that the existence of the object is given only in the perceptive consciousness, philosophic knowledge for Kant "was altogether the *Knowledge of Reason* through *concepts*, a knowledge *a priori* of all experience, without any empirical source, inner as well as outer." And yet, whatever we may say as to the objective existence of the forms of intuition and the categories, this is only to emphasize the existence of *concepts*, of which they are the meaning or contents. And these *concepts*, as such, are facts of inner experience. As Beneke says: " How now did Kant attain to these universal rules which he sets up for our knowledge? Since he represents these as having objective validity, as truly grounded in the nature of the human spirit, incontestably he got them only through *inner* experience." Again, "only through inner self-consciousness also could Kant become certain of the power which brings the human mind to the forms of its knowledge; only through the inner self-consciousness could he become certain of the process through which knowledge is builded by these powers." And again, "only on the basis of inner experience can philosophy, and in particular scientific knowledge of the human soul, be established with certainty and steadfastness." All this is only to give special prominence to inner consciousness as a fundamental datum of individual experience. And with the recognition of this fact we reach the fundamental starting point of Beneke's psychology and philosophy.

CHAPTER II

BENEKE'S SYSTEM IN GENERAL OUTLINE

I THE SCOPE AND METHOD OF PSYCHOLOGY

§ 11. *Starting Point of Empirical Psychology*—We are now in a position to see what Beneke regarded as the starting point of Empirical Psychology. That starting point is individual experience, and the insight that individual experience is a perceptive and a conceptive consciousness existing combined in an organic unit. Accepting the English interpretation of experience as phenomenalistic, and agreeing with Kant that only through the unity of the soul is any experience at all possible, Beneke still finds himself at variance with both his English and his German predecessors. With the English, as to their exclusively introspective or descriptive method, resulting in the conception of the soul as a hierarchy of faculties; with Kant and his successors, as to their purely *a priori* method, resulting in the conception of the soul as a purely formal or abstract unity. His own method entirely precludes the criticism to which both the above are open, and particularly the criticism of Mr. Spencer on Kant, that the latter treats only of the adult consciousness. Beneke insists on the distinction between the developed and the undeveloped soul. It is the developed soul that distinguishes its experiences into the twofold aspect of perceptive and conceptive consciousness, or outer and inner experience. It is the developed soul alone that can be for us the source of our knowledge of the undeveloped soul. Beneke again and again insists on this. " Experience," he says, "gives us at first only what happens." Therefore "we are able to acquire a knowledge of the processes of the soul not yet attained to consciousness only *through our knowledge of the developed soul.*"[1] Of our own earliest development self-consciousness tells us nothing; and whatever we know of others (children) is very obscure.

§ 12. *Subject Matter of Empirical Psychology*—The immediate subject matter, therefore, of empirical psychology is to be found in the facts of inner experience. This of course is not to exclude the investigation of the facts of outer experience, so far as these are phenomena in consciousness. But the reason for beginning with the facts of inner experience is that if we are to know anything, we must be able to know the nature of knowledge itself. True knowledge, Beneke concedes, can be grounded only on perceptions. But this means that such knowledge is the *experience* gained from perceptions by comparison, and the interpretation of one in terms of another. And this knowledge falls entirely within the realm of ideas, or what has been called inner experience or self-consciousness. And it has become possible only in so far as the soul has taken up and held fast the elements supplied by perception. Hence, urges Beneke, "knowledge must bear on it indelibly the stamp of the soul, and the highest basis for knowledge of the soul, will be the highest basis for all knowledge."[2] The immediate object, therefore, of psychology is what one finds in his self-conscious experience. And "however difficult may be the *real* limitation of the soul in comparison with what is corporeal, for *the grounding of our knowledge*, we have a thoroughly clear and sharply defined boundary line. The object of *psychology* is all that we apprehend through *inner* perception and sense.

---

[1] *Lehrbuch der Psychologie als Naturwissenschaft* (2d ed., Berlin, 1845), § 21. This edition is the basis of all the following references to the *Lehrbuch.*

[2] *Erfahrungsseelenlehre als Grundlage alles Wissens* (Berlin, 1820) pp. 7–8.

What we apprehend through *outer* sense is at least not at once and immediately suitable to be consumed by it, but if it is to become useful for it, must be explained upon the apprehension of the first species."[3]

§ 13. *Psychology as Distinguished from Other Sciences*— If now, in accordance with the previous analysis, we regard all that we perceive through outer sense as pertaining to body, and all that we perceive through inner sense as pertaining to soul, psychology distinguishes itself from the outer sciences, not as to its *immediate* object, for in each case is the immediate object a form of conscious experience, but as to its indirect object, or that to which conscious phenomena are referred. But while the *observation* of outer sense experience is thus given over by psychology to the outer natural sciences, the *knowledge* resulting from such observation, since this, as an existence, is found in *inner experience*, is still regarded by it as falling entirely within its province, and so open to its criticisms and explanations.

§ 14. *The Method of Psychology*—Beneke's conception of empirical psychology as a natural science will be considered at length when we come to the detailed statement of his psychological system. Here it will suffice to note his contention that, while psychology is to be distinguished from the external sciences by its *indirect object*, in *method* it is one with the natural sciences. That is to say, the methods of induction, hypothesis, and experimentation, which have proved so valuable in the external sciences, are equally applicable to the facts of inner consciousness.

II THE RELATION OF SOUL AND BODY

§ 15. *To Adopt the Method of Natural Science is not Ma-*

---

[3] *Lehrbuch der Psychologie als Naturwissenschaft* (Berlin, 1845); *Einleitung*, § 1.

terialism—Beneke is careful to insist[4] that the adoption of the method of Natural Science is a very different thing from Materialism. Indeed the analysis of experience just completed, resulting in the conception of it, in any given case, as an individual consciousness which discriminates itself into a twofold aspect, inner and outer experience, brings forward in an entirely new light the long vexed question of the relation of body and soul. Beneke has discussed this question in an elaborate work of some three hundred pages, "*Das Verhältniss von Seele und Leib*," and has also set forth clearly his main conclusions on this point in the *Lehrbuch*.[5] His great merit in this respect is the thoroughgoing fashion in which, on the basis of the critical philosophy, he disposes of the opposition as conceived by the old metaphysics, and the new light in which, in disposing of the older materialistic parallelism, he places our conception of the relation between corporeal and physical processes.

§ 16. *Opposition of Soul and Body one in and for Consciousness*—The first point upon which Beneke insists is the fact that *the opposition of soul and body*, matter and mind, is one which *exists alone in and for consciousness*. Theory of knowledge, at its phenomenalistic stage, has analyzed experience into a perceptive and a conceptive consciousness, into an outer experience and an inner experience. But this, it is to observed, is a classification as to *contents*. The content of the perceptive consciousness is *things;* the content of the conceptive consciousness is *thoughts*.[6] Outer experience is knowledge of material objects in space. Inner experience is knowledge of immaterial thoughts in time. Now a given

---

[4] Cf. *Die neue Psychologie*, p. 6.   [5] *Lehrbuch*, Ch. I, part III.

[6] I have occasionally used the terms "perceptive (or objective) consciousness," and "conceptive (or subjective) consciousness," to cover the distinctions of "external sense," and "internal sense," or what Beneke denominates simply as "outer experience," and "inner experience."

"thing" of the perceptive consciousness, and a given "thought" of the conceptive consciousness, may each become the object of other conscious states or ideas. In other words, we may have knowledge *about* a thing, which originally formed part of the perceptive consciousness, and knowledge *about* a thought, which originally formed a link in the conceptive consciousness; and both kinds of knowledge, as being ideas in the restricted sense of the term, it is to be observed, fall entirely within the conceptive consciousness.[7] And so, not only so far as these two original forms of consciousness, but also so far as these two forms of conceptive consciousness, are clearly opposed, they are opposed, as Beneke says, in the one case, "for our apprehension," in the other for our "*knowledge* grounded thereon."[8] Since outer experience, as to content, yields knowledge of objective material things, and inner experience, as to content, yields knowledge of subjective immaterial things, even if provisionally, on the basis of the Kantian theory, we regard both forms of knowledge as phenomenalistic, we may define both body and soul, matter and mind, in the manner already foreshadowed: "All that we perceive through *self-consciousness* pertains to the knowledge of the soul, and all that we perceive through *outer sense* pertains to the knowledge of body."[9]

§ 17. *Psychical and Corporeal Processes, Likewise Oppositions in and for Consciousness*—But now the perceptive consciousness reveals more than things—it discloses among the coëxisting material phenomena movements, events. The conceptive consciousness reveals more than thoughts—it discloses among its successive ideas relations. By observation of the changes among material phenomena, we arrive

---

[7] That is, strictly speaking, "knowledge *about* things," forms the "ideas of sensation" of Locke, and "knowledge *about* ideas," his "ideas of reflection."

[8] *Lehrbuch*, § 43.   [9] *Lehrbuch*, § 43.

at knowledge of the laws of Matter (Body); by observation of the order of succession and coëxistence among our thoughts, we arrive at knowledge of the laws of Mind (Soul). Both kinds of knowledge tell us of processes; on the one hand of the process of corporeal evolution, on the other of the process of psychical development; and just as we so sharply distinguish the perceptive from the conceptive consciousness, likewise we regard the utmost opposition as existing between these two processes. Thus again, for our apprehension, Motion, the form of activity of Matter, becomes so utterly opposed to Thinking, the form of activity of Spirit, that philosophy has even gone to the length of regarding these two forms of activity so independent and diverse as to be conceivable *per se*.

§ 18. *Real Relation between Soul and Body*—It is not the intention at this point to attempt a complete answer to the question of the real relation between body and soul, or more strictly of the real real relation of consciousness to an external world. That is the problem for metaphysics, and a problem which, as Beneke conceived it, can be solved only after the preliminary work of empirical psychology is completed. But we may now at least clear the way in part for the metaphysical solution by a juster appreciation of the oppositions just set forth. Philosophers, says Beneke, in criticism of the attempt of the earlier Metaphysics, in their zeal for a deep philosophical knowledge, have carried over what is merely "an opposition in knowledge" to the *Real*, with the result that they have represented the Soul and Body in opposition to each other "*in their inmost being.*"[10] The consequence of this has been that since the experience of every moment reveals body and soul in immediate coherence in one and the same being, and their immediate interaction one upon the other, there have arisen most wonderful hypothe-

---

[10] Cf. *Lehrbuch*, § 44.

ses, such as the "Conscious Automatism" of Descartes, the "Occasionalism" of Geulinx, and the "Preëstablished Harmony" of Leibnitz. But the attempts of Cartesianism (or of modern Physiological Psychology"), to set up the bodily organism as a mechanical automaton, with its fleeting accompaniment of psychical phenomena in mysterious parallelism, or the attempt of Materialism to reduce mental phenomena to vibrations of molecules of the brain, Beneke contends, must remain for ever impossible, just because not only the bodily organisms of other men exist for us merely as phenomena in our perceptive consciousness, but "even our own body, as every other corporeal thing, we apprehend *only through the impress on our senses*, and consequently * * * not immediately as it is in itself."[12]

This argument holds good, also, when we apply it to the opposition between corporeal and psychical processes. Not only is this opposition, as was pointed out, one which exists for our apprehension, but it is also to be observed that "*there is no kind of corporeal process which cannot under certain circumstances become conscious, and as a thing in consciousness (als Bewustes) be directly perceived by us.*"[13] But in doing this it becomes something *psychical*. "Such a revolutionary change of a thing usually not a psychical apprehension to a psychical apprehension*, should be unthinkable in case of *a fundamental opposition in their being;* only the more by this are we brought to the conclusion that *both kinds of powers in their innermost nature must stand very close to each other*, and that for the explanation of their inner coherence and interaction no artificial hypotheses are necessary. What we apprehend of the human body through the

[11] Beneke in the *Lehrbuch*, § 47, note 3, expressly raises the question whether Anatomy or Physiology will ever succeed in demonstrating the parallelism of a thought, or a thought process, with certain molecular conditions of the brain.

[12] *Lehrbuch*, § 48.   [13] Ibid., § 48.

senses, or what we usually call "the body," we have to look on only as the *outward signs or representations* of the inner (*in itself*) being of the body, which just as in the case of the soul, consists of certain *powers and their processes*, which, while they are different from those of the soul, still *in reality* are like unto them."[14]

III THE ORIGIN OF CONSCIOUSNESS

§ 19. *Meaning of "the Origin" of Consciousness*—The analysis just completed gives a new turn to the question of the origin of consciousness. What now, we may ask, is the real meaning of this question? The history of philosophy, if it has shown anything, has shown *all* experience to be a form of consciousness, that is, both outer and inner experience have as their necessary and essential characteristics the grasping of multiplicity as unity. The manifold of sense, the successive series of seemingly discrete elements of the stream of thought, if really manifold, if really discrete, could never constitute experience, as we know it, much less yield consciousness of themselves as manifold or successive. If then we inquire as to the origin of consciousness, this must mean either of two things. First, the question must be as to the conditions and possibility of any experience whatsoever, *i. e.* it must touch the grounds and possibility of both the perceptive and the conceptive consciousness as a whole; or second, it must refer to the conditions and possibility of certain particular facts within either the perceptive or the conceptive consciousness. The former is the truly philosophical, or metaphysical question; the latter may be regarded as a purely scientific one.

§ 20. *Metaphysical Method of Solution*—In attempting to account for experience as a whole, Beneke shows himself in the widest opposition not only to the method of Materialism,

---

[14] Ibid., § 48.

but also to the *a priori* method of procedure as employed in the metaphysics of Kant.

His opposition to the materialistic method has already been shown in his criticism of the automaton theory. In spite of the great achievements of modern science, and of the value of the atomic theory as a working hypothesis, in spite of the valuable results achieved by physiological psychology,—the criticism of Berkeleian idealism, and the demonstration by Theory of Knowledge of the conscious character of all experience, must ever prove valid against crude Materialism. To begin with a universe of Matter existing in a real Space and thus attempt to account for all experience, is not only to fail on such a basis to render an intelligible account, but is also to ignore the very data of experience. That which is fundamentally given in experience is not a material universe in itself, existing in space, but the two forms of consciousness so often alluded to. This is why Beneke urges that, if we attempt to ask concerning the Real, " we must recognize that there can be no doubt that beyond all comparison we know better what a Soul than what a Body is."[15] Simply because body, so far as it is known, or enters into our experience, is already in the realm of the Soul, as forming part of our conscious experience. This too is why he points out that, as against Materialism, "the history of psychology shows one is not in a position ever to explain or to construct even the slightest thing in the development of the soul out of that which is material. And not only this, but there can also be no doubt that this will be just as little possible for all future time."[16]

Beneke's opposition to the *a priori* method of Kant touches the very heart of his conception of psychology as a natural science. According to Kant, empirical psychology was to have its principles predetermined and handed over to it by

---

[15] *Lehrbuch*, § 47, note 1.   [16] *Lehrbuch*, § 45.

metaphysics. The new philosophy, on the other hand, contends for the reverse process. The starting point for *all* scientific investigation is experience, and experience in the sense of the immediate consciousness of the individual. The *a priori* forms of Kant, the intuitions of space and time, and the categories of the understanding, are philosophical concepts which, as concepts, may or may not at a given time be present in the immediate inner conscious experience of an individual. But "all philosophical concepts are truly products of the human soul; and only by a knowledge of the manner and way they originate in it can they gain their greatest clearness."[17] Only when we first on the basis of scientific observation and experiment have examined into the nature of the origin of our ideas, shall we be able to pass on their validity or ascertain clearly their presuppositions. And if this be so, not only is psychology the science of inner experience, but "the rest of the philosophical sciences consequently are all nothing more than an *applied psychology.*"[18]

§ 21. *Psychological Method of Solution*—Turning now to the second sense in which the question of the origin of consciousness may be understood, we find Beneke proposing this problem with an insight which, if it had been open to English thinkers, would, we must believe, have given an entirely different character to British traditional philosophy. The attempt to explain any given idea or consciousness as a whole as the mere product of the material, or, as Beneke puts it, the attempt "to carry the psychical development back to the corporeal," has already been shown to be invalid, so far as we mean by the material or the corporeal, the "*extra-mentem*," or that which lies beyond all conscious experience, the so-called "real." But now there is an entirely new sense in which we may regard the psychical as a product of the corporeal. Any particular fact of the con-

---

[17] *Kant und die philosophische Aufgabe*, pp. 89–90. [18] Ibid., p. 91.

ceptive consciousness, *i. e.*, any given memory, concept, etc., may depend for its existence on certain material conditions. In other words, the condition of the existence of a given subjective fact may be some given material *thing*. For example, I should never gain the concept *book*, nor the memory of any particular book, unless certain objects had once prefigured in my individual experience as a distinct part of my perceptive consciousness. But then *a material thing*, in this sense, *is already a part of my conscious experience*, and as existing within the conscious realm, already exists in the realm of the soul. The origin of ideas, then, in the sense of the material conditions of their existence, is to be understood, not as a question as to the direct dependence on, or a certain correspondence to molecular brain structure, of which we know absolutely nothing, but as a question concerning *the dependence of one form of consciousness on another*, both of which being directly present to clear conscious experience, and both of which, leaving their distinct traces in memory, lay themselves open to subsequent analysis, by virtue of which the whole psychical process of development or evolution of the soul may be traced. It is at this point that Beneke's thought shows itself in most striking contrast with the philosophy of Mr. Herbert Spencer, to which his philosophy offers surprising points of agreement. His grasp of the conception of consciousness as an evolutionary development is most complete, but his great difference from Spencer is that the evolutionary process is regarded not as one of a mysterious unknowable, nor as one of a real physical process in a real physical universe,[19] but as a soul process, taking

---

[19] Mr. Spencer's well-known contention that his philosophy justifies neither idealism nor materialism falls to the ground in a remarkable admission made by Mr. Spencer himself in a reply to certain criticisms of Prof. Watson; "Our Space Consciousness: A Reply" (*Mind*, July, 1890). After arguing at considerable length that the great body of our space knowledge lies latent in our inherited nervous structures, Mr. Spencer says (p. 323) : "*Of course the interpretation takes*

place entirely within the perfectly knowable realm of the soul.

§ 22. *Source of the Notion that Self-Consciousness is Materially Conditioned*—The origin of the notion that ideas are materially conditioned is not far to seek. The history of philosophy has shown how the French sensationalists in following Locke carried back all ideas to sensations; how Condillac expressly says:[20] "Our ideas are nothing more than transformed sensations;" how Diderot implied the same in his dictum[20] that "every impression which cannot find an external and sensible object to which it can establish its affinity is destitute of signification." We have seen how for Hume, too, ideas were but faint copies of original impressions. What now is the ground of this procedure? What has given occasion to this view, Beneke declares, is "only the greater *Clearness* and *Definiteness* which the presentations of the physical have, for a person unused to self-apprehension, over the presentations of the psychical."[21] But this superior clearness and definiteness of sense-perception, as we shall later find Beneke demonstrating, and as modern psychology has clearly made out, is not explicable as the unaided result of the exciting stimulus. The content of our perceptive consciousness owes its distinct, definite character in no small degree to the representative element present in it, that is, to the reinforcing effect of sub-conscious elements excited from

---

for granted the existence of objective space, or rather of some matrix of phenomena to which our consciousness of space corresponds. Manifestly the hypothesis that a form of intuition is generated by converse with a form of things, necessarily postulates the existence of a form of things." And Mr. Spencer attempts to justify this wholesale admission by a mere *tu quoque!* For he adds: "With this admission, however, may be joined the assertion that the Kantian hypothesis tacitly, though unavowedly, inconsistently makes the same assumption."

[20] Quoted by Sir William Hamilton: *Metaphysics* (Bowen's Edition, Cambridge, 1861), p. 402.

[21] *Lehrbuch*, § 46.

memory. Beneke consequently urges as to the vividness and clearness of the contents of the perceptive consciousness that " this superiority still is grounded *purely subjectively* (*i.e.*, in the nature of our power of intuition), and its being turned over to the '*real*' or *objective*, can be justified by nothing."[22] Beneke goes even further. He claims that the apparent superiority in vividness of the facts of the perceptive consciousness is only an accidental circumstance, and that " by long-continued and judiciously conducted practice in. the apprehension of the psychical product and its effect, an equally great, yea, even a still greater clearness and definiteness can be obtained."[23]

IV THE UNITY OF MIND OR CONSCIOUSNESS

§ 23. *Beneke compared with English and with German Thinkers*—In psychological method and in metaphysical conclusion Beneke occupies a position somewhat midway between the English psychologists and the abstract German thinkers typified by Fichte, Schelling and Herbart. With the English psychologists his point of contact is his thoroughgoing reliance on introspection, with the difference that he carries introspection farther, and supplements it by hypothesis and experimentation. From the Germans his point of departure is his thoroughgoing attempt to deny not the ab-

[22] Ibid., § 46.

[23] Not to mention the superiority acquired by mathematical concepts and judgments, compare for an interesting experimental confirmation of a like superiority in the case of mental images, Meyer's account of his visual imaginations (Quoted by James, *Psychology*, Vol. II, p. 66). Meyer says: " With much practice I have succeeded in making it possible for me to call up subjective visual sensations at will. . . . I can now call before my eyes almost any object which I please, as a subjective appearance, and this in its own natural color and illumination; I can see them almost always on a more or less light or dark, mostly dimly changeable ground. Even known faces I can see quite sharp, with the true color of hair and cheeks." Most of these subjective appearances even left after images. See the page mentioned for further valuable details.

solute necessity of unity to experience, for to this he agrees, but that this unity may be conceived otherwise than as a concrete organic unity,—a complete concrete psychical organism. In this connection it is to be remembered that, while there are certain points of substantial agreement between Beneke and Herbart, and while the latter was not without influence in moulding some of Beneke's views, still only by the most utter disregard of his concept of the soul as a "Simple," as maintained in his Metaphysics, was Herbart able to set it forth in his psychology, as he practically did, as a single concrete psychological mechanism.

§ 24. *The Soul as a Hierarchy of Faculties*—Beneke's view is in striking contrast to the Lockian concept of mind, which had resulted among English thinkers in the extremest form of "faculty psychology," with its hierarchy of relatively independent agencies, through the activity of which all mental phenomena were to be explained. Beneke shares[21] with Herbart the merit of freeing psychology from the evil consequences of this misconception. He himself regarded this improvement as the first and chief point in the thoroughgoing reform in psychological method which largely through his own and Herbart's efforts was beginning to be instituted in his day. The basis for this improvement, Beneke recognized, was laid by Locke in dealing a death-blow to "innate ideas," and in showing that all concepts arise by abstraction, and in last analysis grow out of presentations which have reached the intuitive stage, whether these presentations be in either outer or inner experience. But the advantage so gained was nullified by the retention of innate "faculties." The phenomena of the developed soul, or adult consciousness, it is true, allow themselves to be discriminated into certain psychical forms,—presentations, memories, imaginations, con-

[21] In the *Lehrbuch*, § 12, note, Beneke expressly gives Herbart credit for his part in the new reform.

cepts, judgments, reasonings, volitions, etc. But because these various forms of consciousness can be brought under a single class concept, is no justification for referring them to a single "faculty" or power of the soul. Such faculties are naught but hypostasized class concepts, important enough purely as descriptions, but valueless so far as pretending to be a profound account of the nature of the soul. The true method of procedure, insists Beneke, is first to ask how these psychical forms arose in experience. Though we find them in the fully *developed* soul, " it by no means follows that faculties, or powers, must belong to the *as yet undeveloped* soul, and be contained *preformed* in these psychical forms."[25] Beneke thus is one of the very first to insist that psychology must take more account of the evolutionary process involved in the development of all psychical forms. For as he says, with the emphasis of italics, " *Of all these forms which we perceive in the developed soul, it is admitted that they are produced through a very long series of intervening processes.*"[26]

§ 25. *The Soul as a Simple, or Abstract Unity*—Beneke's view, again, is in striking contrast with that concept of the soul which reduces it to a mere undifferentiated abstract principle. We have seen how Kant analyzed all experience into a form of consciousness, and how Beneke attached the utmost importance to the distinctions of outer and inner conscious experience. If now we inquire as to the justification for applying the term consciousness to the twofold forms of experience, we shall find the essence of consciousness indicated even in the etymology of the word which stands for it. It is *knowing together.* Only so far as the manifold of sense is apprehended as one, only so far as successive feelings are apprehended in a thought which grasps their re-

---

[25] *Lehrbuch*, § 10.   [26] Ibid., § 10.

lations, can experience, such as we know it, be possible."[27] Both in the perceptive and in the conceptive form of consciousness then are we able to analyze out a "something" over and above the diverse constituents of the given experience; a "transcendental unity," without which, as constituting its absolutely necessary condition, experience of any kind is utterly inexplicable. But there is great danger of going wrong in the way in which we may understand this "something." How unrelated sensations, discrete, isolated impressions, could ever constitute experience, it is true, is perfectly unintelligible. But, on the other hand, an "empty Unity," a common being into which single things disappear

[27] Compare an interesting foot-note by Professor James, *Psychology*, Vol. i. (New York, 1893), p. 162, recognizing this "essential character" of experience, and confirmatory of the unintelligibility of regarding experience, or knowledge, as a series of truly distinct and separate elements: "It may seem strange to suppose," the note concludes, "that any one should mistake criticism of a certain theory about a fact for doubt of that fact itself. And yet the confusion is made in high quarters enough to justify our remarks. Mr. J. Ward, in his article Psychology in the Encyclopædia Britannica, speaking of the hypothesis that 'a series of feelings can be aware of itself as a series,' says (p. 39): 'Paradox is too mild a word for it, even contradiction will hardly suffice.' Whereupon, Professor Bain takes him thus to task: 'As to "a series of states being aware of itself," I confess I see no insurmountable difficulty. It may be a fact, or not a fact; it may be a very clumsy expression for what it is applied to; but it is neither paradox nor contradiction. A series merely contradicts an individual, or it may be two or more individuals as coëxisting; but that is too general to exclude the possibility of self-knowledge. It certainly does not bring the property of self-knowledge into the foreground, which, however, is not the same as denying it. An algebraic series might know itself, without any contradiction. The only thing against it is the want of evidence of the fact' (*Mind*, xi., 459). Prof. Bain thinks, then, that all the bother is about the difficulty of seeing how a series of feeling can have the knowledge of itself *added to it !!!* As if anybody was ever troubled about that. That, notoriously enough, is a fact: our consciousness is a series of feelings to which every now and then is *added* a retrospective consicousness that they have come and gone. What Mr. Ward and I are troubled about is merely the silliness of the mind-stuffists and associationists continuing to say that the 'series of states' *is* the 'awareness of itself;' that if the states be posited severally, their collective consciousness is *eo ipso* given; and that we need no further explanation, or 'evidence of the fact.'"

by "fusing," can be, as a later writer has put it, "nothing but a blank featureless identity."[28] Such a featureless identity, Schelling, on the basis of the Fichtean Ego, attempted to establish as the groundwork of all that is,—an absolute identity or indifference. Such a featureless identity Herbart, inconsistently with his psychology, makes the soul, when he says: "The soul is a simple essence (*Wesen*), not merely without parts, but also without any kind of diversity or multiplicity in its quality."[29] But Beneke protests again and again against the attempt to regard "the whole rich manifoldness given in consciousness and in nature" as having "their being and their truth only in and through this poor or perfectly empty Unity."[30] As against Fichte and Schelling he exclaims: "All deduction of *plenum* from a *vacuum*, of the *particular* from an *abstract* that is indifferent to the particular, is a work of the imagination, and a smuggling in by stealth of what has been reproduced from previous experience. Human thinking, of any sort, can only *clear up*, can only make prominent for clearer apprehension, what is already in part included in the material given to it for its consumption from elsewhere. It cannot create out of itself the *content* of a presentation. Only within the manifold can unity be found. Not the manifold within unity."[31] Or, as Beneke sums it up in another place and connection,[32] philosophy

---

[28] Green: *Prolegomena to Ethics* (Oxford, 1890), p. 31, § 28: "It is true, as we have said, that the single things are nothing except as determined by relations which are the negation of their singleness, but they do not therefore cease to be single things. Their common being is not something into which their several existences disappear. On the contrary, if they did not survive in their singleness, there could be no relation between them—nothing but a blank, featureless identity. There must, then, be something other than the manifold things themselves, which combines them without effacing their severalty."

[29] *Text-book in Psychology* (tr. by M. K. Smith, International Education Series, New York, 1891), p. 119.

[30] *Kant und die philosophische Aufgabe*, p. 45.

[31] Ibid., p. 62. [32] Ibid., p. 85.

"dares not wish to be more simple than nature and the human spirit are themselves."

§ 26. *The Soul as a Concrete Psychical Organism*—Beneke's own view of the original nature and being of the soul will be better understood after the detailed statement of his psychology. Here, however, we may indicate the nature of the substitute which he proposes for this "abstract unity," for this "undifferentiated oneness," in which the manifold of experience, as manifold, becomes lost and fused—that indifferentism of Schelling which Hegel characterized as "the night in which all cows are black."[33] Beneke clearly recognizes that "unity," in the sense of the apprehension of the manifold as one, is the form of all conscious experience. But then such unity, so far as known, is an existence for consciousness. It is merely the logical form of the presented contents of experience, and it does not therefore follow that we must because of it accept a fundamental faculty which is *individual or one*, or a power which is *at once all in one* (*Gesammt Kraft*). "The mistake has been made," he says, "that for all soul processes *which agree with one another in form* (for all concepts, desires, volitions, reasoning, etc.), a *single* fundamental faculty or unifying activity has been supposed, through which they become produced. But because they are one *logically*, or *for our perceiving*, it does not at all follow that they must also *in reality*, or *in their psychical foundation*, be one (an *identical oneness*)."[34] "The (developed) soul," he continues,[35] "has not *one* understanding, one power of judgment, one will, etc., but *thousands* of powers of understanding, of powers of judgment, of powers of will." Thus every cognition, every judgment, every emotion, every volition, is a distinct and separate process in itself. There is no *one* same 'faculty,' 'form,' or 'category,' which presides over

---

[33] Cf. Schwegler, *History of Philosophy*, p. 318.
[34] *Lehrbuch*, § 11. [35] Ibid., Note 2.

each and every particular experience of the varied kinds named, and into which all such particular experiences coalesce or become submerged in an indifferent identity. Nor is to say this to take away unity from the soul, but only to understand that unity, not as an abstract logical form, but as a concrete interconnection of parts constituting a system. For "of course everything in the soul is intimately united in a single whole or one. But not of this *universal* oneness is it treated here, but of the *immediate* oneness of *truly particular forms* one with another."[36]

The unity of the soul, then, as conceived by Beneke, takes on a new form as compared with the prevailing way in which it tended to be regarded by the German successors of Kant. The soul for him is "a *throughout immaterial* being, consisting in certain fundamental systems, which *not only in themselves, but also with one another, are in their true inwardness one*, or form just *one being*."[37] Thus, for the "simple soul" of the Herbartian, for the "abstract unity" of the Fichtean or Schellingian, Beneke substitutes the conception of the mind or soul as a concrete psychological organism. And this organism, as being an interrelated system, is in the truest and most intelligible sense of the word *one*.

[36] Ibid., Note 3.   [37] *Lehrbuch*, § 38.

CHAPTER III

Beneke's Empirical Psychology—Introduction

I PSYCHOLOGY AS A NATURAL SCIENCE

§ 27. *Introduction*—The empirical psychology of Beneke, we have already seen, starts with a very advanced conception of the nature of man and of knowledge. It accepts the *naïve* attitude of phenomenalism and looks upon the individual as distinguishing himself into a two-fold form of experience, and regards both these kinds of experience as consciousness. By outer experience it means that panoramic series of pictures which in the individual's waking moments is incessantly passing before him; or, not to give undue prominence to visual phenomena, outer experience includes, as Hume would put it, also all lively and violent "sensations, passions and emotions, as they make their first appearance in the soul." Visual, tangible, and audible things, then, and in fact all sensations, as they make their first appearance in conscious experience, are regarded as "outer experience." By inner experience, on the other hand, is meant that stream of subjective remembering, imagining, reasoning or thinking, which we are ever conscious of as going on simultaneously with the passing show of the panorama before us.

§ 28. *Inner Experience the Immediate Object of Psychology*—With this insight clearly in mind, we are in a position to appreciate the significance of Beneke's efforts to establish psychology as a natural science.[1] If it was the merit of Kant

---

[1] For a full discussion of this point see *Die neue Psychologie*, Erster Aufsatz: "*Ueber die Behandlung der Psychologie als Naturwissenschaft*," pp. 1–50.

that he brought philosophy back to outer experience, it is Beneke's great merit that he brought psychology back to inner experience. The great success of the method of external sciences had already become demonstrated in Beneke's day. All psychology needed, thought Beneke, for a like success, was, beside a clear concept of its field and scope, the scrupulous use of those very methods which had so greatly aided natural science. This field was inner experience, self-consciousness; but the method of investigation was to be, as against the old metaphysical attempt to construct knowledge "out of mere reason," "out of mere concepts," or through "pure speculation," thoroughly scientific, that is, empirical. Psychology, as well as the outer sciences, was to depend directly and entirely on experience, but the experience which was to be the distinct subject matter of psychology was *inner* experience.

§ 29. *The Objective Method Dealing with the Inner Experience of Others*—In making inner experience the direct subject matter of psychology, Beneke clearly recognized the possibility of two distinct methods of study, due to the fact that the experience with which psychology has to deal may be either the *inner experience of ourselves* or that *of other men*. Against the objective or comparative method, which deals with the experience of other men, certain obvious disadvantages, it is true, may be urged. We as individuals are not in a position to perceive immediately and inwardly that which passes before the minds of others. We are limited to the *outward signs* of their inner thoughts, so that psychological knowledge attained in this way must, it would seem, be and always remain in the highest degree incomplete. At any rate, the knowledge so gained must at the best be a knowledge grounded on the analogy of our own individual experience. And since, "in every other man, every man sees only himself," it is all the more important, to avoid the misinterpretation due to the limitation of our own individuallity, that our own individual experience should be properly and fully interpreted by us. While therefore the psychological knowledge gained through others must always be more or less uncertain because of its indirectness, nevertheless this knowledge, urges Beneke, is not so uncertain as at first appears. The intense interest which mankind have shown in one another, coupled with the desire to learn with exactness what another thinks, feels and wills, has resulted in the formation of a language of signs, which through the coöperation of millions has gained an extraordinary richness. This language, too, through scientific labor, is capable of immeasurable perfection, and indeed, says Beneke, the perfecting of it has already been undertaken with such success and zeal that on the whole, so far as the expression of human language is concerned, very little has been left to be desired.

§ 30. *The Subjective Method Dealing with the Inner Experience of One's Own Self*—While fully appreciating the necessity of putting our purely subjective interpretations to the test of "general assent," Beneke nevertheless believed in the essential superiority of the subjective or introspective method. This superiority lies in the fact that what passes before us *in our own experience* is not only capable of more exact examination, but indeed is open to *direct* inspection or observation. For this reason, particularly in self-apprehension, or inner experience, we have the chief source of psychological knowledge (*die Hauptquelle der psychologischen Erkenntniss*).[2]

§ 31. *Possibility of Applying the Method of the External Sciences to Inner Experience*—I shall not attempt here to follow Beneke through his whole able discussion of psychology as a natural science, mainly because most of his conclusions and arguments have become scientific common-

[2] Cf., *Die neue Psychologie*, p. 14.

places at the present day. It is not too much to say, however, that he is the father of modern experimental psychology, although in the development of this method, his original standpoint and insight, as to the real starting-point of empirical psychology, has unfortunately in too many instances been entirely lost sight of. This starting-point was the phenomenalistic view of individual experience, with the explanation of both the inner and outer forms of which psychology has to do. Against the objection that inner conscious experience is not open to observation and experimentation in the same manner as outer conscious experience, Beneke argued with profound insight. We are apt to overlook the fact that a scientific observer is a *trained* observer. Mere observation of things will not yield full knowledge of them, but only acquired perceptive powers. The botanist in looking at the flower receives perhaps no more stimulation from it than the uneducated man. But how much more in a glance he sees! This is only to show that in outer perception there are varying grades of clearness, definiteness and exactness. But this, too, is true in the case of internal perception. By unnumbered repetition, not only the vaguest, faintest sensation, but all the facts of inner sense can be brought to like grades of clearness, definiteness and exactness. And this is true even of the most fleeting ideas.

The experimental method has become so firmly intrenched in psychology in these days that there is no need to repeat the arguments by which it was first established. It is exceedingly interesting, however, to note some of the various ways in which Beneke, as one of the earliest advocates of the method, thought it could be employed. "We are able, for example," he says, "to think upon a circumstance after previously we have thought upon a like one, or of something differing from it in this or that degree, and with this or that degree of attention, during this or that length of time."[3]

[3] *Die neue Psychologie*, p. 20.

Continuing in this strain, he suggests other varied experiments with memories, percepts and feelings, so commonplace at the present day as to need no further mention.

II GENERAL NATURE OF THE PSYCHOLOGICAL PROBLEM

§ 32. *The Problem Stated*—The first point in attempting to solve the fundamental psychological problem, the alterations in consciousness, is clearly to conceive the nature of the problem and the data with which we may begin. Beneke, familiar as we have seen with the results of Locke, Berkeley, and Hume, accepted as data that description of individual experience which regarded it as distinguished into two great orders or series of phenomena, the so-called lively or vivid *impressions* of Hume—outer experience, and the so-called fainter internal *ideas*—inner experience. Impressions distinguish themselves into a multiplicity of objects or things, the investigation of the coherency and relations of which constitutes the natural sciences; while ideas distinguish themselves into memories, imaginations and cogitations (meaning by this latter, concepts, judgments and reasonings), the discrimination and description of which constitutes the work of descriptive psychology, and the origination of which in any given individual constitutes the work of education in the broadest sense of that term. On this basis, then, of a clear circle of changing impressions and a concomitant stream of fleeting ideas, theory of knowledge continues its work. Its task is not to *describe* the contents and coherences either of the circle of impressions or the stream of ideas, but taking in hand some *individual experience*, to *interpret* the exact manner in which the alterations in that conscious experience take place, and just how a given individual experience grows to be what it is.

§ 33. *Previous Attempts at Solution of the Problem*—The failure of previous philosophers either to conceive clearly the nature of the psychological problem as involved in the philosophical interpretation of experience in its twofold aspect, or to furnish an adequate solution of it, was fully appreciated by Beneke. If the individual experience is to be distinguished into two forms or aspects, a perceptive consciousness and a conceptive consciousness,—a realm of things, and a realm of thought,—then an adequate psychology will account for the nature growth, and implications of both these forms of experience.

But, as to a psychology of the perceptive consciousness, the shortcomings of the earlier English philosophers have already been pointed out. Locke never got beyond a purely descriptive faculty psychology of the most pronounced type, and, as a matter of fact, never seemed to grasp vividly enough the distinction of inner and outer experience so often contended for in these pages. For the "Ideas of Sensation" and "Ideas of Reflection" of Locke, while apparently distinguishing experience into external and internal perception, seem only too frequently in his pages to be ideas in Hume's restricted sense of the term, and so fall entirely within the conceptive consciousness or inner experience; while the differentiated picture or aggregate of things which at any moment constitutes a given individual's *percept* of the outer world, seems again and again to be entirely passed over or lost sight of by him. Berkeley, again, while showing a distinct recognition of the perceptive consciousness, and referring to it as consisting of "*real things*," in spite of his recognition that in all developed visual perception we go beyond present sense, not only fails to show how the alleged "aggregations" of sensations could ever constitute "things," but avoids the necessity by supposing them to be directly "imprinted on the senses by the Author of Nature." Finally Hume, in his account of the nature and origin of impressions, also fails to render a satisfactory account of the perceptive consciousness. Instead of starting with the complex consciousness given in immediate experience, Hume almost at the outset assumes that it is made up of certain "simple perceptions or impressions" such as admit of no distinction or separation. These simple impressions, it is true, are regarded as somehow combined into "complex impressions," which may be distinguished into parts. But why a given individual's perceptive consciousness at a given moment is such a complex as it is, why it is made up of lesser groups or complexes of simple impressions, are questions which Hume, in respect to the perceptive consciousness, does not pretend to answer. As to the origin, too, of impressions, Hume is equally silent. "As to those *impressions*, which are from the senses," he says,[1] "their ultimate cause is in my opinion perfectly inexplicable by human reason, and 'twill always be impossible to decide with certainty, whether they arise immediately from the object, or are produced by the creative power of the mind, or are derived from the Author of our being."

It was the defects of these English doctrines of impressions as a theory of perception, or as even a description of the perceptive consciousness, that awoke Kant from his dogmatic slumber. The attempt of Hume to describe the perceptive consciousness as a mosaic of disconnected sense impressions continuously undergoing lightning-like kaleidoscopic changes, only served to force into clearer relief as the essential nature of such consciousness its characteristic of multiplicity *in unity*. A psychological atomism of the Humean type not only fails as a true description, but could never serve as an intelligible fundamental foundation for experience in the form which the perceptive consciousness reveals it to be. Momentary experience, as we know it, is manifestly and obviously the apprehension of the manifold as one.

[1] Hume, *Treatise of Human Nature*, p. 84.

The absolute condition of the very existence of the perceptive consciousness, Kant therefore urged, is the "transcendental unity," or synthetic activity, which stands over and above the multiplicity given in sense perception and gives unity to it.

Further, as to a psychology of the conceptive consciousness, the shortcomings of the earlier English psychologists are likewise manifest. We need not review here the views of Locke and Berkeley, but may proceed at once to their outcome in the psychology of Hume. However willing Hume was to regard the coëxistences and successions of simple impressions as entirely *fortuitous*, he readily allowed that, in inner experience, simple ideas (supposed to be fainter copies of original simple impressions) are *not* entirely loose and disconnected subjective facts which somehow fall into groups by chance. The imagination in its workings seems, he says, to be "guided by some universal principles, which render it in some measure uniform with itself in all times and places."[5] The same simple ideas, experience frequently shows, fall regularly into complex ones. How could they do this unless there were some kind of union among them, some associating quality, by which one idea naturally introduces another? But this "uniting principle among ideas," in Hume's hands, finally resolves itself into a mere tendency of the imagination to feign, becomes a "fiction of the mind," and as the mind or soul itself is ultimately explained away by Hume, the relations among ideas are ultimately made to depend on those relations of contiguity and succession in the perceptive consciousness, which were left over by Hume *unaccounted for*, and as "perfectly inexplicable."

It was likewise the defects of this earlier English doctrine of the interconnections of ideas which Kant attempted to

---

[5] *Treatise of Human Nature*, p. 10.

remedy. "Whatever may be the origin of our ideas, * * *," he urges, "they must all belong to inner sense. All knowledge is, therefore, at bottom subject to time as the formal condition of inner sense, and in time every part of it without exception must be ordered, connected and brought into relation with every other part." * * * "Now if I draw a line in thought, or think of the time from one day to another, or even think of a certain number, it is plain I must be conscious of the various determinations, one after the other. But if the earlier determinations—the prior parts of the line, the antecedent moments of time, the units as they arise one after the other—were to drop out of my consciousness, and could not be reproduced when I passed on to later determinations, I should never be conscious of a whole; and hence not even the simplest and most elementary idea of Space and Time could arise in my consciousness."[6] That is to say, Kant here again would emphasize the unifying activity as the peculiar function of mind, and this unified character—multiplicity in unity—as the peculiar characteristic of all experience, outer or inner.

The whole point of the criticism, so far advanced as to previous theories regarding both perceptive and conceptive consciousness, and the point which marks in particular the advance on Hume, centres about the synthetic activity which reveals itself as the dominating characteristic of experience. This much, at least, is clear gain from Kant, that the elements of experience are more than absolutely independent, disconnected psychological atoms or sense impressions. So far as a manifold of sense has conscious existence at all, it appears to a percipient Ego or Self, the essential characteristics of which are, on the one hand, the ability to synthesize the manifold given it in experience, and so apprehend it

---

[6] *Critique of Pure Reason* (Watson's *Selections*), p. 57.

as one, on the other hand, the ability to *preserve* and *reproduce* its separate experiences in time. And only on the basis of such a hypothesis is explicable the simultaneous presentation of the multiplicity of coëxistence and the multiplicity of succession as wholes.

§ 34. *The Problem as Conceived by Beneke*—Beneke's conception of the true nature of the fundamental psychological problem takes him back to this point in the Kantian criticism. The whole effort of German philosophy subsequent to Kant had turned upon the definition or understanding of the transcendental unity or Ego, which Kant had implied as the fundamental condition of any experience whatever. And in the hands of Fichte, Schelling, and, as Beneke thought, Hegel, this Ego had been made out to be little better than a "a poor, empty unity," a logical abstraction spun out by the old reprehensible metaphysical method of explicating concepts. But the starting point of psychological investigation is not the preconception handed over to it by metaphysics of the Soul, either as a "Simple," or as a "Transcendental Ego," innately furnished with forms of intuition and with categories. The real starting point is Experience, inner and outer, and ultimately the immediate object of psychological inquiry must always be the investigator's own conscious experience in its twofold aspect. Experience, so conceived, reveals itself as a series of kaleidoscopic changes; and only when we have first investigated how the alterations in the consciousness constituting an individual experience are to be conceived, shall we be able to reach any conclusions regarding the original nature and being of the Soul.

There are two points, therefore, in the investigation of the psychological problem, upon which Beneke, in his criticism of previous theories, strenuously insists; first, the individual character of the problem, and second, the necessity of an exacter insight into the meaning of changes in consciousness. As to the first point, Beneke insists that preceding theories have been "entirely too general" in character, "and therefore incapable of being applied to the explanation of individual experiences."[7] As to the second point, the preceding prevailing doctrine, in its explanation of changes in consciousness, had never gotten beyond "what was figurative." "It has spoken," he says,[8] "of a 'slumbering,' of an 'awakening,' of a 'being awakened,' of ideas, of an 'association' among them, etc. But it tells us nothing of the *precise thing which happens* in these processes."

What now is "the precise thing which happens" when changes in the content of immediate conscious experience take place? There are three things, says Beneke, which psychology wants to know about the alterations of consciousness: (1) *Exactly what is changed* in a presentation when from being a conscious state it becomes an unconscious trace, or that which is capable of later re-entering consciousness as a memory; (2) *Exactly what change takes place in this trace* or tendency, when it is restored to consciousness; (3) *Exactly what is imparted* to it on its being combined with others.[9]

III BENEKE'S DOCTRINE OF TRACES

§ 35. *Transition*—Before entering directly upon discussion of the fundamental psychological problem as outlined by Beneke, it is first necessary to explain what is perhaps the most important part of his whole psychology, his general doctrine of the persistence of psychical forms.

§ 36. *The Fact of Persistence and How Known*—No facts of consciousness, it is generally conceded, are more in evidence or are more obvious than the constant reproductions of original experiences which, in their phenomenal aspect at

---

[7] *Lehrbuch*, § 86.   [8] Ibid., Note.   [9] *Cf. Lehrbuch*, § 86, note.

least, have gone by forever. No facts of consciousness, nevertheless, have more failed of proper interpretation than these. It is the custom of modern psychologists of a certain type, in their almost ludicrous efforts to conform to a so-called rigorous "scientific method," to begin their work with elaborate descriptions of the human nervous organism. Then, on the basis of this preliminary *preconception*, they endeavor to interpret not only the facts of memory, but those of all conscious life. Not so with Beneke. He as a psychologist who has risen to the conception of experience as a form of consciousness, and who, having completed his *description* of the facts, is ready to *interpret* them, founds his data on the twofold form of conscious experience so frequently insisted on. Beginning with this as a basis, so obvious when attention is properly called to it, as to become a postulate, the true psychologist next looks whether there are any other facts which come home to consciousness with like coercive or axiomatic force. Such a fact is the *unconscious persistence of psychical forms*. All memories, considered as psychical existences, and at the moment of their forming part of an individual experience, are facts of *inner experience*. Any memory, considered as to *content*, reproduces either an original fact of outer experience, or an original fact of inner experience. The reproduction of previous experiences, inner or outer, as memories, is so obvious and constant a fact of every day life that, as Beneke says, it is only too surprising that preceding speculation had never supplied an adequate theory of its nature and significance. "Reproductions of presentations, and other psychical forms repeat themselves in every moment of our waking lives, so that in consequence, there lies before every man immeasurable riches of facts of this sort; and one therefore would think that the theory on this point must long ago have raised itself to the highest clearness and exactness."[10]

[10] *Lehrbuch*, § 86.

How now do we know of the unconscious persistence of psychical forms? Simply through the *fact of reproduction*. Conscious experience shows itself to us as an almost continuous process of *change*. But we soon find that this change is not so far-reaching a matter as at first appears. It is not so much a change in things or being; it is only change *in conscious activity*. And we soon find that "everything which has once been formed in the human soul with any completeness, *preserves itself, even after it has vanished from consciousness, or from an active psychical form into unconsciousness or the inner being of the soul, from which it thereupon can later emerge into a conscious psychical form or be reproduced.*"[11] Thus then in view of these most obvious and universal facts of experience, we are led to believe in the unconscious persistence of psychical forms, and the basis of our knowledge of such persistence is the obvious *fact* of reproduction.

§ 37. *Nature of Unconscious Persistence*—Beneke, however, thinks that we may do more than merely affirm that persistence of some sort is a fact of conscious experience; we may say something as to the nature of this persistence. A psychical form, or conscious phenomenon, which is not now present to consciousness, which in other words has sunk into a subconscious or latent state, may be regarded from two points of view—in reference to the original conscious experience, inner or outer, of which it is the vestige, and in reference to the reproduced conscious experience, of which it is the foundation. This "unconscious persistent," in relation to the psychical product which continues in this manner to exist inwardly, Beneke calls "a trace" (*eine Spur*); and in relation to the psychical product which is formed upon it as a foundation, or which can proceed from it, a "rudiment," or "tendency" (*eine Angelegtheit*).[12]

[11] *Lehrbuch*, § 27. [12] Cf. Ibid., § 27.

As to the nature of "traces," so far as they are unconsciously persisting things, Beneke boldly asserts that they are *psychical existences*. Traces, of course, in that they are unconscious, cannot, he grants, be represented or known immediately as they are in themselves. But "*the trace is what lies between the product of a soul activity* (e. g. a sense-perception) *and its reproduction* (e. g. as a memory); and since both these acts are *psychical* acts, we have a right to represent also the trace only in *psychical*[13] form."[14]

§ 38. *The Philosophical Significance of Memory*—Beneke's doctrine of the persistence of psychical forms becomes of the greatest importance because of the profound psychological significance which it assigns to the facts of memory. Facts of the individual's outer experience (Things), and facts of the individual's inner experience (Ideas), are apprehended in consciousness not only as single objects, but possess varying grades of vivacity, clearness, intensity, activity and rapidity of development. Undoubtedly a scientific man when he perceives a given flower actually sees more at a glance than would an uneducated individual looking at the same object. Undoubtedly, too, the *idea*, which the scientific man has of this flower, is livelier, clearer, more active (when actually present) in determining the complexion of the succeeding states of inner thought, and characterized by more ramifications or interconnections, than that of the uneducated man. How, then, a given perception, or a given

[13] To the contention that retention is a purely physiological fact, Beneke would reply as follows: If we ask concerning the "where" of a given trace the answer is that it is "nowhere." For as with the soul in general, so with all its parts, they are "nowhere." If again we ask whether "traces" are not somehow attached to the bodily organs, the answer is plain. Bodily organs exist too as facts for the perceiving consciousness, as part of the content of outer experience, and at most can only be said to be *parallel* to subjective facts. In no intelligible sense of the word can traces be said to be "attached" to bodily organs.

[14] *Lehrbuch*, § 29.

idea, or even the perceptive consciousness of the individual as a whole, has attained to its present vivacity, clearness, intensity, etc., are questions towards the solution of which, insight into the nature and significance of memory affords invaluable aid. Beneke therefore maintained that his theory was important for two reasons. In the first place, a direct consequence of the doctrine that "traces are not cast out of the soul by their becoming unconscious" is to emphasize that any given fact, either of outer or of inner conscious experience, is not to be explained as a ready-made product stamped clearly and immediately in all its completeness on the blank passivity of the soul; but rather that such individual facts, as well as the momentary perceptive consciousness as a whole, has its origin and its definite character determined in no small measure by the mass of memories which form the subjective possession of the soul. In the second place, the doctrine is important in forcing to a clear issue the real problem which presses psychology for solution. It is not the persistence of psychical forms that needs explanation, since we may explain this on the ground that "*What has once happened continues to exist until it is destroyed again in consequence of some special cause.*" [15] What then must yield to explanation, urges Beneke, "is not the retention but *the becoming unconscious of what previously was conscious.*" [15]

Beneke's doctrine of traces thus brings us back to that conception of the fundamental psychological problem with which we started, and especially to the discussion of those specific questions which must be answered if the alterations of consciousness are to be explained in any profound sense of the term.

[15] *Lehrbuch*, § 28.

CHAPTER IV

THE PSYCHOLOGY OF INNER EXPERIENCE

I GENERAL INTRODUCTION

§ 39. *Transition*—We are now ready for the scientific investigation of experience—inner and outer. These two forms of experience, we have seen, are the real data for scientific inquiry; both are to be regarded as forms of consciousness; and for the understanding of both the doctrine of the persistence of psychical forms is of vast significance.

§ 40. *Knowledge both a Product and a Process*—We must notice, however, at the outset, a distinction which has proved revolutionary in modern psychology—that between knowledge as a *product*, and knowledge as a *process*. Beneke, it would seem, was one of the first psychologists to appreciate the full significance of this distinction. "All psychological observation," he says, "is confined to consciousness, and the process of awakening to consciousness, consequently, as that in which *consciousness first takes place* (which therefore precedes in *un*-consciousness), is necessarily withdrawn from our observation."[1] Thus, so far as we treat a "thing" of the perceptive consciousness, or a "thought" of the conceptive consciousness, merely as a product, that is in respect to its *presented content*, we never get beyond the realm of a purely descriptive psychology. Only when we attempt to get at the *presentative activity* back of the given thing or thought—at the process back of the product, do we get on

[1] *Lehrbuch*, § 87.

the track of what really will throw light on our fundamental problem—the changes and alterations of consciousness. But inasmuch as the process of knowledge is apparently shut off entirely from direct observation, it would seem as though psychology had here struck a chasm which it could never bridge.

§ 41. *Changes* TO *Consciousness, and Changes* IN *Consciousness*—While it is true that if the psychologist can never get beyond immediate consciousness, the task of psychology must prove hopeless, it is also true that there is a real way out of this difficulty. At no point in his whole philosophy does Beneke show himself profounder than in this distinction: If the process of awaking *to* consciousness is not open to direct observation, the process of arising *in* consciousness is. And, since every conscious change, once clearly experienced, remains as a trace in the inner being of the soul, we may by recollective reflection on previous experience see exactly how changes *in consciousness* have taken place, and thus, if there be any, discover the laws which govern these changes. Consequently, may we not further, on the basis of the facts so ascertained, argues Beneke, "make the inquiry whether we are not in a position to explain also the mounting from *an unconscious to a conscious* state in accordance with like laws?"[2] In consequence of this distinction, the investigation of inner experience naturally comes first. For the facts of outer experience, as Beneke alleges, are in part the product of stimulants taken up from the outer world, but the facts of inner experience are forms of consciousness directly depending on other immediate forms of consciousness (those of immediate outer experience).

[2] *Lehrbuch*, § 87.

II INNER EXPERIENCE: ORIGIN OF INDIVIDUAL FACTS

§ 42. *The Facts of Inner Experience*—Inner experience reveals itself as a series of ever-shifting states or pulses, each of which has a definite individual character. To these individual states or pulses, in order to distinguish them from things or external impressions, we may apply the generic term thoughts, or ideas. Ideas then, further, differentiate themselves into certain specific kinds: imaginations—reproductive (*i. e.* memories proper) and productive, concepts, judgments, and reasonings. Beneke distinctly recognizes each of these kinds. Memory in general, as we have already seen, is merely the persistence in the inner being of the soul of what has once formed part of the clear conscious experience of the individual. Properly speaking, however, Beneke contends, there is no such thing as memory in general. There are only specific memories, for "*every individual presentation has its own particular memory.*"[3] Memories proper then are imaginations of the individual reproductive type. But so-called productive imaginations, Beneke holds, are also reproductive. That is, " in respect to *content* (the material) of their representation, they are merely reproductive; productive, entirely in respect of their *form.*"[4] These two types are, in the wide sense of the term, reproductive imaginations (*Einbildungsvorstellungen*). The existence, moreover, of concepts (*Begriffe*) judgments (*Urtheilen*), and inferences (*Schlüsse*), are all fully and specifically recognized by Beneke as facts of inner conscious experience.

§ 43. *The Origin and Growth of Ideas*—Whatever we may say ultimately and finally as to the nature and meaning of conscious experience as a whole, the scope of the method of investigating the origin and growth of the facts of inner experience, as was shown in the discussion upon the origin of

---

[3] *Lehrbuch*, § 103.   [4] Ibid., § 109, note 2.

consciousness,[5] has for psychology been clearly made out. We saw then that the question of the origin of ideas is one "concerning *the dependence of one form of consciousness upon another*, both of which being directly present to clear conscious experience, and both of which leaving their distinct traces in memory, lay themselves open to subsequent analysis, by virtue of which the whole psychical process of development or evolution of the soul may be traced." It is just in virtue of this fundamental fact,—viz., that everything that has once taken place in experience with any measure of clearness persists in the soul as a memory, that we are able to trace out the exact process by which the given occurrence has come to pass. With this method in mind, we proceed, therefore, to the examination of those changes which take place entirely within the conscious realm.

(1) *Memories*—If we inquire first as to the origin of the simplest facts of inner experience—memories of particular objects—we must note first what, in Beneke's psychology, becomes demonstrated of all the facts of inner experience, that they all depend on certain original experiences in the perceptive consciousness. The person who has never seen an alligator can have no memory of an alligator. The person who has never heard the music of the hautboy can have no memory of those particular sounds. Beneke thus agrees with Hume "that any impression either of the mind or body is constantly followed by an idea, which resembles it, and is only different in the degrees of force and liveliness." But while with Hume, "the chief exercise of the memory is not to preserve the simple ideas, but their order or position,"[6] with Beneke memory, in the sense of persistence, assumes a clearer function, and is indicative of an important psychological process. My memory of the face of my intimate

[5] Chap. II, § 21. [6] *Treatise of Human Nature*, p. 9.

friend, whose photograph I see every day, is a more vivid, clearer inner experience, than my memory of the face of some casual accuaintance, whom I have beheld but once or twice. Why? Because I have seen my friend's face as pictured in the photograph a thousand times, my acquaintance's once. Each time I have seen the former, that conscious experience in becoming unconscious has become a trace. These unconscious traces in my soul, being precisely similar, or almost so, all tend to fuse, and represent themselves in consciousness as a single distinct act. If then memories gain in clearness and definiteness through unnumbered repetitions of the original experience which they represent, it is only because of the fusion which has taken place among these separate traces in consequence of the mutual attraction due to their similarity.

(2) *Concepts*—We may inquire now as to the manner in which and the materials out of which concepts arise. Suppose there were presented to my visual consciousness either simultaneously or in immediate succession the following objects: A piece of coal, a clump of soot, a lot of pitch, some ink, a raven, and mourning clothes[1]. There would irresistibly arise in inner consciousness the concept "blackness." Now in each of these things, so dissimilar as a whole, there were certain constituent *parts* common to all. As each of these

[1] In this whole section I have availed myself of illustrative material and precisely formulated statements given in a most valuable little exposition of Beneke's system by Dr. G. Raue: *Die neue Seelenlehre Dr. Beneke's nach methodischen Grundsätzen in einfach entwickelnder Weise für Lehrer bearbeitet.* This book was afterwards enlarged and improved by J. G. Dressler, Director of the Normal School at Bautzen, Beneke's leading follower. It is the book that has done most to make Beneke known to German teachers.

An English translation of this work was made by some unknown person in 1871. Morris in one of the supplementary notes to his translation of Ueberweg's History, cites (Vol. II., p. 285) this work as a translation *made by Raue* of Beneke's *Lehrbuch der Psychologie*. Raue's work was really written in German, and is an original exposition of Beneke's system.'

things was passed before me, the dissimilar elements occurred but *once*, whereas that which was *similar* was repeated *six* times. As the coal passed before me it left its trace in the soul; then the soot, the pitch, and the remaining things likewise. These traces, because of their similarity, instantly attracted each other, or fused as one object. And in proportion to their greater frequency, the common elements were reproduced or represented more strongly and clearly than those peculiar to each of the stated objects. In this manner, then, experience shows concepts first arise.[8]

A like process is at work in the formation of higher concepts. Suppose by the method above explained, I had already acquired in separate ways the concepts, blackness, redness, blueness, greenness. Let some one now, by means of symbols or otherwise, simultaneously or successively arouse in my consciousness these several concepts. Instantly there arises a new concept, a higher one, which I learn afterwards to designate as "color." Hence we reach this general conclusion: "CONCEPTS *arise in the human soul because the similarities in different notions of individual objects (Intuitions) mutually attract each other and fuse together into one whole; and as concepts so formed have also points in common, they in turn coalesce, and hence arise* NEW *and continually* HIGHER CONCEPTS."[9]

(3) *Judgments*—When once a concept has been produced, in consequence of the law of persistence of psychical forms, it continues to exist in the inner being of the soul. Suppose

---

[8] "When, therefore, there are no intuitions, there can be no concepts answering to them. Hence a man born blind has no concept of 'Color,' although he knows the name; the man born deaf has no concept of 'Sound,' nor can such persons ever obtain these concepts. Similarly those who live in equatorial regions are destitute of the concept 'Ice,' nor had Luther any concepts of coffee, tobacco, steam-engine, etc."—G. Raue, in his "*Elements of Psychology, on the Principles of Beneke*" (English translation, Oxford 1871), p. 35.

[9] Raue's *Elements* (*op. cit.*), p. 37.

now, having acquired the concept "blackness," I am again shown the objects mentioned above. Instantly I say: "These things are black." It would be possible to show by thousands of instances that "*when we perceive anything, as a rule a concept* rises into consciousness in addition to that *perception.*" Again, if the word red or black is mentioned, I instantly think, "This is a color." In other words, instances are equally numerous, in which a *higher* concept is summoned into the mind along with another. We mean by judgments, then, cases where either a like concept is called into consciousness along with a (simple) perception, or a higher concept of like kind along with another concept. And here again the essential thing to notice is the attraction of like for like and their fusion.

(4) *Inferences*—The psychological process involved in "drawing a conclusion" is thus stated by Dr. Raue, one of Beneke's earliest and most enthusiastic followers:

"In the human soul there are very often *several* judgments conscious at the same time. Take the judgments:

> All men are mortal
> A Moor is a man

Here we have three concepts side by side, *man, mortal, Moor*. While the first judgment affirms 'mortality' of *all* men, *i. e.*, of the whole compass of that concept, the second declares that the Moor is included in that compass.

"What takes place? 'Man' and 'Moor' are similar concepts, for Moor is but another name for man—it only signifies a particular kind of human being. Hence these two concepts will coalesce, but in such a way that Moor will remain present to consciousness. In fact this concept is *forced* with special strength upon the consciousness, the consequence of which is that not it, but 'all men' is obscured, and almost vanishes from consciousness. The movable elements which kept it consciously present are withdrawn from the latter, and are attracted to the more strongly emphasized term 'Moor.' Hence the only thing the dissimilar concept 'being mortal' can do, is to attach itself to the term Moor, now *vividly* conscious: and so the inference (the inferring judgment) is drawn—(Therefore) *the Moor is mortal* also.

"If in two judgments there is a total want of similar concepts, though they may coëxist in consciousness, yet they can give rise to no new judgment, no conclusion, no inference. Suppose for instance,

>The bird flies
>The fish is aquatic

Here each is *outside* the other, and no inference is possible in such. As the concepts in the judgments, iron is hard, and honey is sweet, can never coalesce, so neither can the former.

"*When therefore two judgments are rendered* SIMULTANEOUSLY *conscious, and in them are contained similar concepts together with one* DISSIMILAR *one, the similar concepts fuse together and a new judgment is produced; because the* DISSIMILAR *concept must attach itself to that one of the similar concepts which in one of the judgments has been brought definitely and prominently into consciousness.*"[10]

§ 44. *First Fundamental Psychological Process*[11]—The examination of the facts of inner experience, as above set forth, therefore, seems to yield a fundamental law governing the formation of the psychical forms found in inner experience. This law, however, Beneke contends, is more than a mere descriptive "law." It is in fact a real fundamental psychological *process* unceasingly at work in the life of the human

---

[10] Raue's *Elements*, pp. 43-44.

[11] For Beneke's statement of the four fundamental psychological processes, see the *Lehrbuch*, Chap. I, I: *Grundprocesse der psychischen Entwickelung.*

soul. It is given by him as the fourth of his "fundamental processes," and is stated as follows:

"*Like products of the human soul, or similar products, according to the measure of their similarity, attract each other or strive to enter into closer union with each other.*"[12]

III INNER EXPERIENCE: A CONTINUOUS PROCESS OF REDISTRIBUTION

§ 45. *Introduction*—Having completed now this review of the individual facts of inner experience, resulting in the discovery of a fundamental psychological process underlying their formation, we must turn attention next to two other important aspects of this form of consciousness. Inner experience reveals itself at once as a continuous process of change, and also as a series or chain of associated ideas. Hence arise two fundamental psychological questions. The first is twofold: a) when once either a perception or an idea has sunk into an unconscious state and so become a trace, exactly what change takes place in it by virtue of which it is restored to consciousness?; b) why should an idea that is immediately present in conscious experience ever become unconscious at all? The second fundamental psychological question asks concerning the connection between ideas: since a given perception or idea shows itself in experience to be connected with a thousand different associates, why is it that in the succession of ideas, a given psychical form at certain times summons in its wake one particular associate rather than another?

§ 46. *Alteration in Inner Experience a Change in Activity* —Inner consciousness is never continuously one individual

---

[12] *Lehrbuch*, § 35. Raue called this formula the "Law of the *Mutual Attraction of Similars.*" Beneke regarded the process as requiring almost no elucidation, because there lie open to immediate observation such abundant instances of the process, not only in its result but also in its happening.

substantive state, whether memory, concept, judgment, etc., in the unchanging contemplation of which it has become utterly absorbed. Inner consciousness, to be sure, can become submerged, as it were, in a long train of thinking on one distinct topic; but, generally speaking, it is always a fleeting series of subjective facts in which memories (proper), concepts, judgments, etc., each follow close upon the heels of the other with unceasing rapidity. If now we accept the contention so far made, that "*in general what has once been formed in our soul with a certain degree of completeness can not become lost again*,"[13] and that "*the source or origin of the powers and faculties of the developed soul is to be found in the traces of the earlier aroused psychical developments*,"[14] this continuous alteration which our self consciousness shows, becomes understood in a new light. Since the soul is stored with the records or memories of its previous experiences, change in inner consciousness then is a change "only in activity" (*nur die Erregtheit*).[15] The absolute condition of retention or unconscious persistence is certain original clearly conscious experiences, perceptive or conceptive. The condition of recall is that these unconscious forms be actively excited or aroused.

§ 47. *Beneke's Doctrine of "Movable Elements"*—If now we inquire why any particular subjective fact occupies at the immediate moment the theatre of inner consciousness, the question is one as to how this given fact became actively aroused. When I look at the photograph of my friend there instantly flashes into my mind, *i. e.*, there engages my immediate inner consciousness, either a memory of my friend's face, or some fact or circumstances which in my past experience have been associated with him. When, as stated a moment ago, I looked at pitch, ink, soot, a raven, etc., in-

---

[13] *Lehrbuch*, § 28.   [14] Ibid., § 31.   [15] Ibid., § 27.

stantly there arose in my inner consciousness the concept
"blackness;" and this was followed by the judgment, "these
things are black." When, too, my mind, *i. e.*, inner consciousness, momentarily becomes centered on the memory of
my friend's face, instantly there is suggested or arises into
active consciousness, a number of successive subjective
facts, which may happen to come in the form of memories,
judgments, or inferences, relating to my friend. These instances, which of course might be multiplied indefinitely, all
go to show that all conscious appearances forming part of
the content of the total momentary percept called outer experience, as well as all facts of immediate inner experience,
have effective power to bring trailing into immediate clear
conscious activity, certain psychical forms which, the instant
before, were utterly outside clear conscious experience, or,
in other words, were existing as unconscious or inactive
traces. What then is the meaning of this power of conscious
forms, already present in immediate experience, to call up
and make active other forms? It can only mean, contends
Beneke, that the stimulating forms actually yield up or transfer certain "movable elements," or stimulants, which prove
effective in making consciously active those forms to which
they become transferred. "Traces or unconscious psychical
forms consequently," he says, "become conscious or active
psychical forms, because there *flow over to them from those
forms already active*, elements suitable to effect this mounting to active consciousness."[16] This is Beneke's doctrine of
movable elements, which, as will be shown later, plays so important a part in his system. These elements, besides
"movable" or "balancing elements" (*beweglicher oder aus-
gleichungselemente*) are also called by him, because of their
function, "elements of consciousness" (*Bewusstseinele-
mente*).[17]

[16] *Lehrbuch*, § 89.   [17] *Lehrbuch*, § 89, note 2.

§ 48. *Immediately active inner Consciousness the Resultant of a Dynamic Process*—That limited span of ideas or thoughts which constitutes the immediate inner consciousness of the moment, Beneke therefore regards as a sort of momentary state of equilibrium brought about by the distribution or diffusion over a certain area of the soul, as it were, of certain movable or balancing elements, toward stimulation by which the unconscious, that is, inactive traces in the inner being of the soul are ever striving. Or to put it in his own words, "Traces or rudiments are not indeed *cast out of the soul* by their becoming unconscious, and must therefore also take part in the *universal balancing* of the movable elements for which all the psychical forms of our being are striving."[18] We see then why certain memories, concepts, judgments, etc., are continually re-arising in consciousness. Immediately active inner consciousness, as Beneke interprets the facts of the case, is a continuous readjustment or balancing process—a perpetual alternation of disturbances of equilibrium and compensating balancings or adjustments. Consciousness thus, in the sense of knowledge, is both product and process—static and dynamic. So far as we regard active consciousness as a substantive state, *i. e.*, as unity embracing multiplicity, we are emphasizing its static condition or phenomenalistic aspect, which is confined entirely to the side of *presented contents*. But the static condition, or knowledge as a product, is the resultant of two factors—on the one hand, the psychical form, or trace, which is aroused from the inner being of the soul, on the other, the movable elements or stimulants which are transferred to it from some actively aroused form of consciousness. Thus so far as we regard active conscious forms as such resultants, we gain an insight into the dynamic aspect of consciousness, or knowledge as a *process*. When

[18] *Lehrbuch*, § 89.

therefore we regard some conceptive form of consciousness as directly depending for its activity on some other form of consciousness, perceptive or conceptive, we must not fall into the error of supposing that Beneke in claiming that something real, from the percept or concept that sinks into obscurer consciousness, is actually transferred to the form of consciousness that gains in clearness, means to say that any part or portion of the presented contents of the form or presentation, becomes transferred in its qualitative aspect *as presented contents* to the latter.[19] Not only the forms of inner

---

[19] It is to be regretted that in the only serious critical, though brief, estimate we have in English of Beneke's psychological views (G. F. Stout: "Herbart compared with English psychologists and with Beneke," *Mind*, January 1889), misapprehension on this point should have led to severe criticism of Beneke. Mr. Stout says, (p. 23): " Many of Beneke's hypotheses are no doubt wild and untenable. But the general conception of the working of the psychological mechanism through which presentations disappear and reappear, or wane and wax in distinctness, seems to have a firm basis in fact. I do not mean that the theory of transferable elements can be in any way justified. What I refer to is the general principle that the rising of one presentation is so correlated with the sinking of others, and *vice versâ*, that the whole process can best be formulated for psychological purposes as a transference of something from the presentation which wanes in distinctness to that which waxes in distinctness. This something we may regard either as a reality or as a fiction, and we may call it attention or psychical energy, or by any other convenient name. But we must not, like Beneke, regard it as a constituent element of the presented content. Nothing is ever transferred from one presented content to another. A presentation becomes more or less distinct as more or fewer qualitative details become distinguishable in it. Now it is obviously untrue that the qualitative details of one presentation ever become transferred to another when the latter become clearer in consequence of the former becoming obscured." Certainly it is a grievous mistake to regard Beneke as contending for any such view as that just stated. Every conscious appearance or presentation, Beneke continually contends, is a product whose factors are always, on the one hand a primary power or group of primary powers (the essentially psychical elements), on the other, certain stimulants, which so far as their being is concerned in respect to the soul, may be external or internal. It is either these primary powers themselves, or the stimulants which have been appropriated from without and made a permanent possession of the soul, that form the transferable elements. This indeed is the basis for the profound distinction between Beneke and the English associationists. With the latter it is *sensations* that are

experience (ideas), but also those of outer experience (percepts) are to be regarded in one aspect as phenomenalistic *products;* and so *what actually becomes transferred* from the exciting form of consciousness is *some part of its factors*, which to be sure, on the representative side of consciousness, may qualitatively re-present precisely what it was on the representative side of the original stimulating percept; but then this only becomes *known* to a *third* conscious experience, which analyzes out the common elements of the two preceding experiences.

§ 49. *Why Forms Immediately Present in Inner Consciousness become Inactive*—The second form of the main question so far discussed, touching the reason why an idea immediately present to inner experience ever sinks out of active consciousness, is easily answered. If a given idea (whether image, concept, judgment or inference), has risen into active consciousness by virtue of a certain gain or stimulation of movable elements, it becomes inactive again, or a mere trace, by suffering a corresponding loss of those elements. If, in the case already cited, the judgment—"These things are black," is instantly followed by the judgment—"Black is a

---

aggregated and segregated so as to give rise to all the higher and varied complex forms of experience. With Beneke it is what lie back of sensations, and make them possible, that become associated. Beneke recognized that even could we penetrate in consciousness to the most elementary ground of all things, the atom, we should only reach "*elementary appearance*," and we must still look back of this for its producing factors (compare *Metaphysik*, p. 122). With this conception of factors there is of course a way out out of the difficulty as to the doctrine of transferable elements. Mr. Stout fully recognizes this himself when he continues: "Only when we disregard presented content, and merely formulate the mechanical connection of mental processes in its quantitative aspect, do we find a legitimate scope and meaning for the conception of a transferable somewhat continually redistributed within the mental system. From this point of view, however, the conception is certainly of value, and it is to be preferred to Herbart's theory of conflict." Certainly this is the point of view which Beneke both in spirit and expressly held. Compare *infra*, § 66.

color," this is because the movable elements which had been at work rendering the concept "blackness" active, have again become transferred with the effect of arousing or exciting into active or immediate clear consciousness the concept "color."

§ 50. *Second Fundamental Psychological Process*—The obvious conclusion from these facts of inner experience is that the alteration in activity revealed in inner experience, is best conceived to be in the nature of a balancing process —in one case, "a partial discontinuance of stimuli,"[20] in consequence of which a psychical form becomes a memory or trace; in the other case, a compensatory restoring of stimuli, in consequence of which it again enters active consciousness. The second fundamental process of conscious experience, then, may be stated as follows:

"*In all psychical combinations, at every moment in our lives, there is an active striving towards a balancing or equalizing of the movable elements contained in these combinations.*"[21]

IV INNER EXERIENCE: AN ASSOCIATION OF IDEAS

§ 51. *Introduction*—Having seen that in general an idea is roused into active consciousness because of the transference to its unconscious trace of certain movable elements, we must turn now to consider the specific question why in a given case a particular idea actually aroused in consciousness becomes supplanted by one particular idea rather than any other with which it has been frequently associated. As this question of the direction of changing consciousness involves the nature of the connections between ideas, the latter problem is considered first.

[20] *Lehrbuch*, § 88: "A *partial* disappearance of this stimulant changes the conscious sensations and perceptions again into unconscious traces or rudiments."

[21] Beneke's "third" fundamental process. Cf. *Lehrbuch*, § 26.

A—THE CONNECTIONS BETWEEN IDEAS

§ 52. *Nature of the Problem*—The real problem involved in the "association of ideas" was very sharply distinguished by Beneke. The inability of the general laws of association as set forth in purely descriptive psychology, to explain the conscious experiences of an individual, has already been pointed out. "It is claimed," says Beneke, "that presentations become associated and awaken one another after the relations of Similarity, Coëxistence and Succession, Contiguity in Space, Causal Connexion, Contrast, etc. But almost every presentation has at some previous time arisen with numerous different presentations in *all* of these relations. Why therefore does the awakening follow, at one time this, at another time that relation, and why does some special one of the many associated presentations become awakened?"[22] To answer this question psychology must know precisely "*what is imparted* to an idea on its being combined with others."

§ 53. *Essential Nature of the Union between Like Psychical Forms*—Since common experience shows us that the union between ideas is of two distinct kinds, that between psychical forms perfectly alike, and that between unlike forms, we must look first to discover the nature of the union between the former. It has been postulated, it will be remembered, that experience is a twofold form of consciousness, outer and inner, and that, as a matter of daily experience, original experiences, whether facts of outer or of inner experience, become reproduced as memories. These memories, so far as memories, are facts of inner experience. Assuming for the moment outer or perceptive consciousness, it is these facts of inner experience that we are trying to account for. Suppose now there is presented to my perceptive conscious-

---

[22] *Lehrbuch*, § 86, Chapter III., on "The Reproduction of Traces," § 86, note 2.

ness for the first time the photograph of a person; or suppose that I hear for the first time some shrill note. The moment the photograph is withdrawn from my field of view, and the moment the note dies away—likeness and note, ceasing from active consciousness, become memories or traces in the inner being of the soul. If now, on a later occasion, I see again the identical photograph, or hear again the same shrill note, again there will be left in the soul traces of these experiences, and these traces will become more numerous in proportion to the number of times the original experience is repeated in exactly the same way. To each of the traces of the photograph above mentioned, no matter if seen a thousand times, Beneke would assign a distinct numerical existence in the inner being of the soul. Upon those numerous traces the psychological process of the mutual attraction of the similar of course tends to operate; but unless this process was supplemented by that of the actual transference of balancing elements, there could arise no real bond or connection between these similar traces. They would remain but a "mere aggregation" of discrete individuals. But these similar traces, Beneke claims, do enter into an organic or vital relation, and this relation or connection is also something numerically real and distinct in the soul. We know this because "even of this *transference of movable elements* from one psychical form to another, traces remain in the inner being of the soul."[23] And it is this transference that becomes the ground of "*all enduring relation.*" That a "permanent linking or union" between these similar forms, then takes place, is due, Beneke concludes, to the "balancing process" by virtue of which the movable elements are transferred from one form to another.

§ 54. *Effect of Conscious Activity on the Inner Character*

---

[23] *Lehrbuch*, § 34.

of the Trace"—A first characteristic, then, of the inner nature of a trace, is this strengthening (*Verstärkung*) or close bond of intimacy which has resulted in consequence of similar psychical forms being aroused to active consciousness. The *second* time my friend's photograph occupied a part of my perceptive consciousness, it, in consequence of the law of the mutual attraction of similars, was immediately attracted towards the *trace* of the original sense perception, the original perception having become a trace by losing part of its stimulation. But not only were the two conscious forms, percept and trace, attracted, but the actively conscious percept, in consequence of the universal balancing process, transferred some of its stimulants to the unaroused trace, and thus tended to make the latter consciously active. When now this virgin trace lapses again into an inactive state, it does not do so unchanged. It has entered into organic relation with the second trace. There has been formed between the two traces a connecting path, as it were, which Beneke regards not as "an *ideal relation*, but as *something real continuously existing in the inner being of the soul.*"[25] This path or connection, too, has resulted from the actual transference of movable elements. And every time a new similar memory has been formed, this process has repeated itself until the thousand traces of the given photograph form a complete organic tissue in the soul's inner being.

Besides this organic union resulting from conscious activity, the trace in its inner nature possesses two other important characteristics, dependent on the *quantity* or number of exactly similar traces. Sense perceptions, as well as other immediately active sense forms, become traces, we have seen, because of a *partial* disappearance of the balancing

[24] Cf. *Lehrbuch*, Chapter 3, IV: *Wirkung der Erregung auf der innere Beschaffenheit des Erregten.*

[25] *Lehrbuch*, § 34.

elements, by the appropriation of which they have become active. This means then that every time an actively conscious form lapses into unconsciousness, "a part of the balancing elements remains behind with the inner trace, or united with it."[26] Thus the greater the number of separate traces forming the given organic aggregate, the greater will be the quantity of balancing elements remaining. The direct and important result of this then is that, since this organism of traces "will afterwards require fewer balancing elements in order to become genuinely conscious," such an organism is brought *nearer the threshold of consciousness.* While a second important effect of the quantity of traces on the connection between conscious forms, is that the union will be most intimate where the greatest number of traces *completely alike* have fused, or better, become interconnected in one organic aggregate.

§ 55. *Effect of the Inner Character of the Trace on Active Consciousness*[27]—The inner being of the developed soul, thus, according to Beneke, is a mass of organized memories or traces. But, if now I have seen the same photograph a thousand different times in precisely the same way, when I recall this object, the separate traces left by the original perceptions do not come trooping into consciousness one after the other. "In consciousness this *aggregate of similars* presents itself as a single act (*Ein Akt*), which, according as the number of these elements is less or greater, gives itself, so far as known, a fainter or stronger character."[28] When therefore the final memory arises in consciousness, although really a manifold, it appears as a unity. But its manifoldness, in which consists its *quality*, is perceived not *immedi-*

---

[26] *Lehrbuch,* § 97.

[27] Cf. *Lehrbuch,* Chap. 3, III: *Einfluss der inneren Beschaffenheit des Zuerregenden.*

[28] *Lehrbuch,* § 95.

ately, or qualitatively, but only by means of its strength or vivacity, i. e., *quantitatively.*

§ 56. *Laws of Quantitative Differences of Presentations*— Two very important laws are to be observed in respect to this quantitative difference of presentations, and to its bearing on the balancing process at work in effecting active consciousness. Although a part of the stimulation remains in connection with a conscious form even when it sinks to a trace, and in consequence, the quantity of traces in a given aggregate requires less stimulation to restore it to active consciousness, nevertheless it is not the total trace (*Gesammtangelegtheiten*), as an aggregate, but the *simple traces* individually, that form the true basis for the balancing or equalizing of the movable elements. Hence results the first law: that "*every aggregate or psychical form contains the more balancing elements,*[29] *the more simple traces it arises from.*[30] But it also results that the greater the number of simple similar traces united in a given aggregate, the greater will be the capacity, so to speak, of this aggregate for the balancing elements. Such an aggregate then tends to draw from the immediately active and stimulating conscious form all its activity, without giving back any in return. Hence the second law: "*The greater the number of simple traces from which a given presentation arises, the more fitted it is to appropriate and hold fast for itself those elements tending to bring about active consciousness.*" (*Erregungselemente*)[31]

§ 57. *Nature of the Union Between Unlike Psychical Forms* —So far the discussion has turned on forms supposed to be perfectly alike. But daily experience reveals cases of immediate connection of percept with percept, percept with idea, and idea with idea, where the connected elements, in pres-

---

[29] That is, plays a more effective part in determining the character of immediate active consciousness.

[30] *Lehrbuch*, § 95.   [31] Ibid., § 96.

ented contents, vary from the closest resemblance to almost total unlikeness. Taking for granted, for the time being, separate percepts or individual intuitions, as well as the interconnected group of things that constitutes the immediate momentary percept of the individual, we may note, as to inner experience, that not all ideas are reproductive imaginations, in the sense of exact "copies" or images of original sense-perceptions or impressions. Inner experience has been distinguished into other psychical forms also—fancies, concepts, judgments, inferences. The idea, therefore, which appears to be immediately associated with any given percept or other idea, may show itself to subsequent reflective thought to have been of any one of these psychical forms. A raven, forming part of the pictured content of my field of view, might instantly suggest to (*i. e.*, make active in) my conceptive consciousness, the memory of another resembling bird; while the judgment, "This raven is black," might arouse the inference, "This raven has as one of its qualities color." Now the connection between all so-called unlike forms is to be explained on this basis of a *partial similarity* of the constituent elements of each. The memory of the piece of coal instantly "suggests" the memory of the raven, because, when these two percepts were originally immediately present in consciousness, elements similar in each were immediately attracted to each other. A like process takes place when any two partially similar ideas of any kind are immediately present in active consciousness. But, in any case, this process of attraction is immediately followed by an actual transfer of "movable elements" between the two like portions. And it is this trace or track, left in the being of the soul by the actual transference of balancing elements from one similar form to another, that is the ground of connection between the forms, and this "connection," as we have seen, is to be regarded not as ideal, but as something real. The connection between unlike forms thus has as its deepest ground the connection between like forms, the like forms being, in this case, like parts or portions of the connected unlike forms.

§ 58. *Relations Between Separate Percepts and Between Percepts and Ideas Strengthened by Repetition*—Where the process of transference is not too rapid, not only traces of the original coëxisting percepts or concepts remain, but there also continues to exist in the inner being of the soul, traces of that immediate flowing over of movable elements.[32] Thus these connections or relations between individual percepts, between individual ideas, and between percepts and ideas, come also to be represented in inner conscious experience. And just as memories of individual percepts are at first less lively than their correspondent percepts, so at first these relations, on the presented side of inner experience, "are of course in and for themselves rather faint; but by virtue of frequent repetition they too are able to attain to *every* grade of strength or clearness (*Verstärkung*), so that they are able to surpass even [the first]" (*i. e.*) those originally given in outer conscious experience.[33] In consequence, then, of these connections formed between forms perfectly alike, and between heterogeneous individual forms of conscious experience, the inner being of the soul becomes one organic tissue of more or less intimately connected psychical forms, which on the presented side of active consciousness appear sometimes as groups of coëxisting, and sometimes as trains of successive, elements.

---

[32] "*Auch das Zugleichfliessen der beweglichen Elemente im inneren Seelensein fortexistirt.*"—*Lehrbuch*, § 34.

[33] *Lehrbuch*, § 308.

B DIRECTION FOLLOWED IN THE TRANSFERENCE OF CONSCIOUS ACTIVITY[34]

§ 59. *Law of the Direction of Consciousness*—Having clearly in mind the nature of the connection between various psychical forms, we are now in a position to understand why a given psychical form, which happens to be present in active consciousness, summons in its wake one particular associate rather than another. Change in consciousness means only change in activity, and change in activity means a redistribution of the balancing elements. But the balancing processes, which give rise to the momentary forms of consciousness, have already set up repeated immediate connections between that form which does the transferring and that which receives the transference. These connections between various forms are more or less numerous and complete. Hence, while the reason in general why an idea is roused into active consciousness is because of the transference to it of certain movable elements, the reason in particular why a specific idea arises is because: "*The movable elements are always passed on from every active psychical form to that which is most strongly connected or is one with it.*"[35]

§ 60. *The Law Applied to the Old Laws of Association*—The law just stated, taken in connection with what has been said as to the nature of the bond of union among ideas, throws new light upon, and puts some real meaning into, the old laws of the association of ideas. In general we may say that "the connection arising through *coëxistence* is stronger than that through *succession:* for the latter arises indeed only through a partial and one-sided coëxistence, namely, in that between the end of one psychical process and the beginning of the following. The connection between the *properties* of

---

[34] Cf. *Lehrbuch*, Chap. 3, II: "*Richtung, in welcher die Uebertragung der Erregtheit geschieht.*"

[35] *Lehrbuch*, § 91.

a *thing* shapes it for our perceiving consciousness, for the most part, as an *observed manifold coëxistence;* the connection of *cause* and *effect,* for the most part, as an *observed manifold succession.* The connection of what is given as joined *spatially,* if it is in general to have place *for us,* requires likewise a coëxistence or succession for our perceiving consciousness; and as to the strength of this connection, therefore, this will depend on *how often* such conscious presentations have been produced by us coëxistently or succeeding one another. *Similarity* becomes analyzed into resemblance and difference, whereby that which is different is given *coëxistent* with the resembling parts; and even the fundamental basis of *permanent* connections between like forms is in a certain measure to be referred to a coëxistence. *Contrast* finally shows itself only by virtue of the similarity which lies at its basis as awakening principle."[36]

[36] *Lehrbuch,* § 92.

CHAPTER V

THE PSYCHOLOGY OF OUTER EXPERIENCE

§ 61. *Introduction*—Beneke's doctrine of the perceptive consciousness brings out most sharply and clearly his psychological method, serving to distinguish it at once from the intuitive empiricism of his English predecessors and the metaphysical abstractness of the Germans. He does not attempt like some of the English to *begin* with simple sensations and by the separation and combining of these try to build up the whole complex mental structure of the soul. Nor does he, on the hand, like some of the Germans, *begin* with the soul as an abstract unity or simple, and, from this metaphysical presupposition, endeavor to deduce or spin out to the minutest detail its complex inner organization. Experience,—outer experience, just as it presents itself to the *developed* soul—is his starting point. Analysis of immediate experience, just as the adult consciousness knows it, *may* lead to the hypothesis of simple sensations or impressions, some such as contended for by Locke, and by Hume; and it *may* lead to the conception of the soul as some sort of a unity. But this much at least we may say, that psychology must not begin with these presuppositions.

I OUTER EXPERIENCE: ORIGIN AND GROWTH OF PERCEPTS

§ 62. *Fundamental Characteristics of the Perceptive Consciousness*—Outer experience, in the sense of the individual's perceptive consciousness, shows itself momentarily as a certain complex, more or less clearly differentiated into lesser groups or individuals called things. These things, so far as they are perceived with some degree of clearness, whether they be visual, tactual, auditory, olfactory, or gustatory, may conveniently be called sense-perceptions, or simply percepts. The fundamental characteristics then of the perceptive consciousness are, first, that perceptions are always knowledge of individual or particular things that are actually and immediately present, and, second, that these particular things are always perceived as existing in space, and, while regarded as being something appearing to us, are yet regarded as having their stimulating cause without us. It is these individual facts of the perceptive consciousness, as well as the perceptive consciousness as a whole (*i. e.* regarded as that total immediate intuition which constitutes the individual's immediate momentary percept called outer experience) which psychology must investigate.

§ 63. *The Origin of Sense-Perceptions*—We have already seen enough of Beneke's general standpoint to know that he does not attempt to trace back sense-perceptions to the organs of sense. Of these the adult consciousness knows *immediately* nothing, except so far as they are *appearances* in outer experience; and, as appearances, or sense perceptions, they are the very things which are under investigation. But even when one has attained the phenomenalistic point of view, it is easy for the unreflective consciousness to persuade itself that its intuitions are ready-made products stamped upon it immediately in all their completeness from without. But careful reflection upon outer experience shows that sense perceptions are really very complex affairs. Perceptions, as well as concepts and the other individual facts of inner experience, are a *growth;* so that percepts may exhibit all grades of liveliness (*Stärke*), fixedness (*Stätigkeit*), clearness (*Klarheit*), and precision (*Bestimmtheit*). "Attentive reflection upon experience as it lies directly before us," says Beneke, "shows beyond doubt that sensuous impressions and perceptions of the *developed* soul are by no means of so simple a nature. The sense experiences of children in the first weeks of their lives are manifestly different from the feelings and perceptions of the developed soul; and people born blind who have regained sight are as little able at first to form perceptions similar to ours."[1] We must therefore look for some further explanation of the clear intuitions of the perceptive consciousness.

§ 64. *Sense-Perceptions as Products of Subjective and Objective Factors*—In accounting for the growth of perceptive knowledge Beneke turns to great advantage his fundamental postulate as to the persistence of psychical forms. There can be no sense experience without a corresponding trace having been left in the inner being of the soul. When therefore similar sense experiences repeat themselves, they in consequence of the law of the mutual attraction of the similar, and the direct transference of movable elements, instantaneously call up into active consciousness all traces of elements similar to those which they contain. This apperceptive mass of traces fuses with the immediately excited sensuous feeling, and to this is due the *clearness* which the sensation on the presented side of consciousness possesses, while the apperceptive mass itself becomes refreshened or strengthened by the additional trace of the immediate perceptive experience. Thus then Beneke contends that "in order to the production of *clearly conscious* sense impressions, to the feeling freshly formed through immediate sensuous excitation, there must come from the inner being of the soul something which *corresponds individually and entirely to this feeling*."[2] And what this something is, the preceding analysis of the facts of inner experience has prepared us to understand. As to the growth of sense-perceptions,

---

[1] *Lehrbuch,* § 53.   [2] *Lehrbuch,* § 54.

therefore, we may observe that "(in the case of the child first awakening to conscious life) the original sense impressions, though they may be *like*, are still *immeasurably fainter* than those of the developed soul. But since like sensuous feelings (e. g. of a color, of a sound) are *repeatedly* formed, and since from all these forms *traces* are left in the inner being of the soul, which then flow over to the like feelings aroused later; as a consequence, these *must continually grow in strength*, and thereby must sense impressions and perceptions of the developed soul contain in themselves hundreds, yea thousands of just these psychical acts which in that original feeling were given only once."[3] "For every sense activity of the developed soul therefore," Beneke concludes, "there must properly speaking be two chief constituents working together: (1) A freshly formed sense impression, and (2) the similar traces contained in the inner being of the soul. Every sense-perception, consequently, however simple it may be in appearance, is *in fact already an infinite complex*."[4]

§ 65. *Nature and Meaning of "Original Sense-Impressions"* —It is obvious, however, that any adequate accounting for the perceptive consciousness must say a good deal more about these "freshly formed sense impressions,"—these so-called "original sensuous feelings" to the hypothesis of which analysis of outer experience seems to force us. While percepts, so far as involving numerous similar traces, may be regarded as a complex, which reveals this qualitative difference on the side of presented contents only quantitatively, that is, by its strength or clearness, there is another kind of qualitative difference directly revealed in immediate consciousness. Even the simplest thing we can imagine is, as to content, a manifold, while the manifoldness of the in-

[3] *Lehrbuch*, § 55.   [4] *Lehrbuch*, § 55, note 2.

dividual things of outer experience as immediately present in the momentary perceptive consciousness, as well as the manifoldness of the momentary perceptive consciousness as a whole, is constantly a matter of direct observation. This differentiated content or manifoldness of outer experience, therefore, demands some deeper explanation, and especially is this true of space perception, so far as involved in that clear circle of visual phenomena constituting the immediate kaleidoscopic field of view. So far as Hume attempted to supply this deeper explanation, he was led to the hypothesis of certain *minima visibilia, minima tangibilia*, and other "simple impressions," to which he assigned both qualitative and quantitative differences. Are the "freshly formed sense impressions" of Beneke to be regarded in the same way? Certainly there seems to be good ground for this assumption, Beneke would maintain, inasmuch as we can actually perceive most minute portions of space, actually feel most minute points, and simultaneously hear faint sounds, one of which obviously is of less volume than the others. The obvious facts of visual, tangible and other forms of sense perception, thus seem all to point to certain minimal forms of sensation or sensuous feeling.

§ 66. *Significance of Original Minimal Sensation as Inevitable Hypotheses*—But Beneke differs from Locke, Berkeley and Hume, both in the character which he assigns to these original simple sense impressions as hypotheses, and also in his conception of the method by which we arrive at the knowledge of them. Simple sensations, as a matter of fact, are pure abstractions which are never realized in their isolated oneness in immediate experience. In their individuality they are not even psychological *appearances*, or products for our outer consciousness. And yet outer experience is obviously a spatial manifold that is irresistibly perceived, as well as conceived, as made up of small portions or spaces. But this is only to say that the soul itself, concretely considered, is a manifold; and we have yet to understand how outer consciousness arises at all. If simple sensations, or outer sense experience as a whole, are the product of impress from without the soul, it is obvious that since observation is confined entirely to consciousness, it is not open to immediate inspection how this change *to* consciousness has taken place.[5] It is at this point that Beneke, with great effect, avails himself of the distinction already set forth regarding changes *to* consciousness and changes *in* consciousness.[6] We have already seen the laws governing changes *in* consciousness. May we not explain changes *to* consciousness by analogy to these? If so, we may note that so far we have seen all psychical forms to be the *product* of factors. All the facts of inner experience, and even the clear percepts of the *developed* soul, have shown themselves to result from a *conjunction* between a trace, on the one hand, and certain stimulating elements on the other. Are we not justified then in regarding a freshly formed minimal impression likewise as such a product?

§ 67. *Beneke's Doctrine of Primary Powers (Urvermögen)*

---

[5] Mr. Stout, in the critical article already referred to (Cf. p. 99, note), certainly does Beneke an injustice when he says (p. 26): "Now, Beneke was anything rather than judicious. He claimed with reason the right of framing hypotheses to explain observed facts. But he pushed his hypotheses far beyond what the exigencies of psychological explanation required. Worse than this, he regarded some of his most arbitrary theories, *e.g.*, the appropriation of stimulants by faculties, as directly based on the evidence of introspection." If this means to say that Beneke regarded the appropriation of external stimulants a matter of direct introspection, this is in error, for Beneke expressly and emphatically says it is impossible to have *immediate* knowledge of the process of awaking *to* consciousness (Cf. *Lehrbuch*, § 87 and 20, also *supra*, § 41). If it means to say that we have a *deduced* or mediate knowledge of this process, reached on the basis of certain immediate knowledge of processes directly observed to take place *in* consciousness, then the "arbitrariness" of the hypothesis is not altogether apparent.

[6] Cf. *supra*, § 41.

—It is this conception of minimal sense impressions as psychical products or phenomena that leads Beneke to the most fundamental hypothesis of his whole theory. In the case of these original sense impressions, Beneke calls that factor which comes from the soul a "primary power" (*Urvermögen*) or faculty; that which comes from without the soul, a "stimulant" (*Reiz*). Since now the soul is continuously being stimulated from without, and since the sense impressions so produced are, in consequence of a partial withdrawal of the stimulation, continually lapsing into traces, the primary powers are, as it were, ever being used up, so that, for the production of every fresh sensuous impression, a fresh primary power is needed. Consequently, argues Beneke, "for the complete explanation of the life of our souls, we must take as a basis just *as many sensuous primary powers (sinnliche Urvermögen)* as in the course of life there have been formed elementary sensuous feelings (*sinnliche Empfindungen*)."[7]

§ 68. *Third Fundamental Psychological Process*—We are now in a position to understand what Beneke states as really the most fundamental of all the psychological processes:

"*Sensuous impressions and perceptions are formed by the human soul in consequence of impressions or stimulants which affect it from without.*"[8]

II OUTER EXPERIENCE: OBJECTIVE RELATIONS OF PERCEPTS.

§ 69. *Introduction*—The most important phases of the psychological problem involved in the explanation of outer experience yet remain to be considered. In the first place, the immediate perceptive consciousness presents itself as a manifold of spatially related elements, and we must, therefore, attempt to determine the nature of the objective rela-

---

[7] *Lehrbuch*, § 56.   [8] Ibid., § 22.   Beneke's "first" fundamental process.

tions among such inter-connected phenomena. In the second place, the mosaic of immediate sense-perception is continuously undergoing kaleidoscopic changes, and we must, therefore, attempt to account for these panoramic transformations. The latter question will be considered in the following chapter.

§ 70. *Nature of the Problem*—Preceding psychological doctrines, we have seen, left entirely without answer the question why external consciousness at any given moment is a certain complex, more or less immediately differentiated into lesser groups or complexes. So far as Hume considered this problem, we have seen that he regarded the immediate manifold of sense-perception as made up of certain *mimima visibilia, minima tangibilia*, etc., but with the result of reducing outer experience to an empirical chaos. "Simple impressions" were regarded by Hume not merely as distinguishable, but, consequently, as separable; and so wide was their separation, and so utter their isolation, as to lead him to say, "I do not think there are any two distinct impressions which are inseparably conjoined."[9] But the inconceivability of how minimal colored points, sounds, touches, etc., if actually entirely separated and discrete, could yield experience or consciousness, such as we know it, only forces to the sharpest issue the question how we are to conceive the connections which we actually perceive to subsist among the manifold elements of sense.

§ 71. *Objective Relations Depend on Original Organic Relations of the Primary Powers*—Beneke's conception of the nature of the objective relations of the perceptive consciousness marks his most characteristic difference from, and great point of advance on, the whole advanced psychology of his day, English and German. Similarly to Hume, we have

---

[9] *Treatise of Human Nature*, p. 66.

found Beneke postulating certain original or freshly formed sense impressions. But even these simple impressions, as hypotheses, are hypotheses of *phenomenal* existences. As phenomenal then they must be regarded as the product of factors, or the result of a process, of which, they if they were actually to enter clear conscious experience, would be the mere elementary *appearance*. When therefore we speak of the perceptive consciousness of the adult individual as having resulted from a long series of infinitely repeated original sense impressions, we must be careful to remember that the real existence or being is, on the one hand, the primary powers of the soul, on the other, the stimulants external to these powers, to the *conjunction* of which simple sense impressions correspond. It is the inevitableness of these hypotheses that leads Beneke's concrete mind boldly to conclude that the soul, before it awoke to consciousness, already possessed an organic structural unity in the shape of these interrelated, numerically distinct, primary powers. For he contends, "these primary powers certainly not only in the organic whole of the soul's being (*im Ganzen des Seelenseins*), but also in the collective activity of each sense, are bound together in the most intimate union; nevertheless they must be regarded as sundered or *separated from one another*, in so far as they are able, on the one hand, to enter the field of sensation, in consequence of special connection with the stimulant appropriated by each, on the other, to persist in this connection in the inner being of the soul."[10] It is, therefore, in virtue of this original organic connection between the primary powers of the different senses, and between the individual's sense system as a whole, that a certain objectivity and reality attaches to the interconnections of the manifold which is immediately and successively presented in our perceptive consciousness.

[10] *Lehrbuch*, § 56.

§ 72. *Objective and Subjective Connections Distinguished*—
These original objective connections involved in immediate
outer conscious experience are of course to be distinguished
from those so-called purely subjective connections which
later in and through experience arise between groups and
series of presentations. While Beneke regarded both as
"*something real* in the inner being of the soul," he nevertheless distinguishes them by the supposition that the former
are originally given, whereas the latter arise through that
balancing process or transference which takes place entirely
within the realm of the individual soul. Thus he says:
"The transference of conscious activity is governed by the
connections between psychical forms, or their *degree of oneness*. But these connections are either *already given originally* (in the soul only between the primary powers of one
and the same system, in the body variously and between
several systems), or are first formed *later* (through the immediate transference of balancing elements)."[11]

[11] *Lehrbuch*, § 308.

CHAPTER VI

Conclusions Relating to both Inner and Outer Conscious Experience

I THE CHARACTER AND KINDS OF ACTIVE CONSCIOUSNESS

§ 73. *Character of Consciousness as Determined by Methods of Excitation*—The most fundamental distinction of immediate conscious experience so far recognized has been that between outer and inner. The basis for this distinction we now see lies in the method of excitation to active consciousness. In general, however, as Beneke points out,[1] we are able to distinguish three modes by which psychical forms are aroused into active consciousness: 1) *purely inner;* 2) *purely outer;* 3) *that through the process of transference or balancing.* In the case of this last method, the direction which conscious activity will take becomes determined by the connections of that group of percepts or ideas which *on each occasion* is *actually present* in immediate active consciousness. The second method, depending on an outer impress or stimulant, is the only one that in and for itself is *without any coherency* with the previous being of the soul (conscious or unconscious), and consequently the only one through which the *direction* of the soul's activity can be directly and arbitrarily changed. The first method, depending on the presence in the soul of *still unappropriated* primary powers, which exert an attractive influence on the similar traces of which the inner being of the soul consists, is the

[1] *Lehrbuch*, § 306.

basis of voluntary action, and so calls for more detailed statement.

§ 74. *The Nature of Voluntary Action*—So far we have learned of two kinds of psychical elements, the original primary powers of the soul, and the stimulants taken up from without. The function of this latter has been, through partial separation from the original primary powers by which they have been appropriated, to serve as "transferable elements," by which, in the ensuing balancing process, other similar psychical forms or powers become aroused. Beneke assigns a like function to some of the still unfilled primary powers. They too can be transferred to similar forms, already existing as unconscious possessions of the soul, and can arouse these to active consciousness. They, thus, are the foundation of voluntary action. "The difference between the two species of elements just mentioned," says Beneke, "shows itself moreover also in the reproductions which manifestly are grounded on them. The enhancing which becomes effected through stimulants (*Reize*) *alone*, is the ground of that *fresher, thoroughly involuntary* arising of perceptions and other psychical forms; that through *free* primary powers alone, the ground of the *intense voluntary* arising; that resulting from the *mixture of both*, the ground of the *usual intermediate* arising."[2]

The essential nature of voluntary action thus consists in being the direct cause either of introducing into active consciousness a form not actually and actively present, or of retaining in active consciousness a form already aroused. The most important function of volition then is in deciding *the direction which active consciousness shall take*. The will is of course *determined*, in the sense that, since the primary powers in general draw to them those similar forms which are most strongly connected, it is dependent on the *inner*

[2] *Lehrbuch*, § 90.

organization of the soul as previously formed.³ But its action differs radically from the involuntary stimulation of the balancing elements, in that the direction of consciousness, when the change taking place results from the transference of balancing elements, is *already predetermined* by the connections of those conscious forms which at the given moment are actually and actively present in immediate conscious experience (outer or inner).

§ 75. *Character of Consciousness as Determined by the Kinds of Primary Powers Active*—Actually aroused sensations, as distinguished for consciousness, that is, on the side of their presented contents, may also be classified with reference to those various sub-systems of primary powers of which the soul is supposed originally to consist. Beneke thus divides sensations into three great classes:[4] 1) *Organempfindungen*, which arise from those specific kinds of primary powers that constitute the five special senses, the characteristics of which are that they " stand immediately open to the outer world," and have corporeal representatives called "organs;" 2) *Vital-empfindungen* (including sensations of heat and cold, pressure, and other partially unknown pleasurable moods, etc.), which for all sensuous primary powers are *alike*, or at least only quantitatively different; 3) *Empfindungen* in the digestive organs and in the rest of the *inner* bodily systems, including sensations which accompany the movements of muscles. Sensations of the third class, Beneke observes, are somewhat intermediate between those of the first and second. Indeed sensations of the second and third classes are not only so much alike for the most part that the same word does service for both, but in general the fundamental basis of their production is the same. " For the stimulants from which sensations of the third class arise, although given immediately in the body, are in like

[3] Cf. *Lehrbuch*, § 306. [4] *Lehrbuch*, § 67.

manner outer to the power (*Vermögen*) *which experiences the sensation.*"⁵

§ 76. *Immediate Consciousness as Determined by the Relation of Power and Stimulant*—Actually present sensations, or, more exactly, any fact of immediate conscious experience, outer or inner, may further be classified for consciousness, as dependent on the quantitative relation between the two factors, power and stimulant, of which it is the product. This relation has no unimportant influence on conscious products, and especially upon what Beneke would term their "form." If we were carefully to examine those changes to active consciousness which take place *in* consciousness, that is those changes which are open to immediate observation, we should find that we might distinguish five different forms of consciousness, attributable to five varying quantitative degrees in which the exciting stimulus and appropriating power may combine.⁶

1. *The stimulation may be partial*—In this case the exciting stimulant, or movable elements, are too weak to fill completely the appropriating trace or psychical form. On the side of consciousness we have the phenomenon of a feeling of *dissatisfaction* or *dislike*, accompanied by a longing for completer stimulation.

2. The stimulation may be *exactly commensurate* with the appropriating capacity of the trace. In this case neither factor exceeds the other. This is the fundamental form for *clear representation*.

3. The stimulant is of *marked fulness*, or *overflowing* without being immediately excessive. This results in an immediate feeling of *pleasure*.

4. The stimulation may *gradually* become *excessive*. The result in consciousness is a feeling of *satiety*, or *blunted appetite*.

⁵ *Lehrbuch*, § 67.   ⁶ Cf. *Lehrbuch*, § 58.

5. An excessive stimulation may combine with an appropriating power *too suddenly*. This sudden overstimulation is the basis of the phenomena of *pain*.

In consequence, then, of this varying relation between stimulant and appropriating trace, Beneke recognizes five fundamental constructive forms, and on the basis of analogy, concludes that these forms prove operative also in the case of the external stimulant (*der Reiz*) and the appropriating primary power (*Urvermögen*). All these conscious phenomena, excepting the second, it will be noticed, are emotional products, although the first, in its aspect of a striving after full stimulation, reveals what Beneke regarded as an essential characteristic of volitional action.

§ 77. *The Threefold Nature of Consciousness*—Notwithstanding his recognition of five fundamental constructive forms, Beneke fully and clearly recognized the essentially similar emotional character of certain of these, and so expressly accepted the threefold classification of consciousness into cognitions (*Vorstellungen*), feelings, (*Gefühlen*),[7] and volitions (*Strebungen*).[7] With Beneke, however, these distinctions are not the most fundamental. The deepest distinction is that between primary power (*Urvermögen*) and stimulant (*Reize*). The primary power, it is true, already implies these distinctions. For originally it is a striving or impulse (*Strebung*) after stimulation. In the appropriating of the stimulant consciousness arises, which, on the side of presented contents, will be either a feeling (*Gefühl*) or a clear presentation (*Vorstellung*), as dependent on the intensity of relation between the two original elements.

---

[7] Beneke's analysis of feeling and volition is really perhaps the most important of his whole special psychology. The general plan of the present work, however, has prevented adequate treatment of these subjects, which must be left to other investigators. Cf. *Lehrbuch*, Chapters 6 and 7; also *Psychologische Skizzen*.

II THE SPAN OF IMMEDIATE CONSCIOUSNESS

§ 78. *Introduction*—Conscious experience, outer and inner, as it reveals itself to the immediate observation of the individual, is exceedingly limited and finite in character. So far as attention is concentrated on visual phenomena, outer experience is never more than that pictorial circle of clear consciousness which constitutes our immediate field of view; while in such a case, inner experience is those immediate images, concepts, or judgments directly aroused by the picture before us. The question here to be considered is not that raised by later psychologists as to how many things can be attended to at once, but rather why in general the limited circle of clear consciousness, outer and inner, does not immediately and clearly represent the whole rich manifold of the soul's being.

§ 79. *The Span of Inner Consciousness*—If, as Beneke maintains, even the poorest equipped human soul contains within it an endless multitude of inner traces, why do not these traces all become conscious at once? In Beneke's opinion, " in and for themselves they could all become conscious at once."[8] But we must remember from the preceding analysis that all conscious or active processes of the developed soul arose from unconscious or unexcited psychical existences, because of a transference to them of certain movable or stimulating elements. There are, therefore, three reasons why all traces do not become consciously active at once:

First,[9] because of an insufficient *quantum* of movable elements. A chief source of internal excitation, as we have seen, is the transference or balancing of the movable elements, but these stimulating elements (largely because of

---

[8] *Lehrbuch*, § 305.
[9] Cf. *Lehrbuch*, § 93, note 2; also, § 220.

the limited character of immediate *outer* conscious experience, the main source of them), are not given in sufficient quantity to go round.

Second,[10] because the *quantum* becomes so *diffused* that none of the forms, even of a closely connected group or series, attains to full (clear) consciousness. It often happens that the transference is not strong enough to bring about complete consciousness. Consciousness varies thus from the perfect clearness attendant on complete concentration, through half conscious states, to that of utter absent-mindedness and perplexing confusion, in which properly speaking nothing is clearly conscious.

Third,[11] because of the *partial opposition* of psychical forms. That totally different psychical forms can exist simultaneously side by side in consciousness is perfectly obvious at every glance of the eye. Our percept of the outer world (outer experience) is at every moment such a unity of differing or opposing forms, while the conceptive consciousness (inner experience) at almost every stage is a conscious state whose characteristic is multiplicity in unity. Opposing or differing psychical forms, therefore, do not, as Herbart claimed, tend to keep each other from rising *to* consciousness, but only limit each other *in* consciousness.[12] That is, while heterogeneous *percepts* remain *outside one another*, their similar elements, in consequence of the first fundamental psychological process, tend to *coalesce*, and so far as they do this, we have a *clearer* consciousness. In this sense, opposing forms exclude each other, but they do it *in consciousness*, and by drawing attention to *clearest* consciousness.

Insufficient quantity, then, stimulating of elements, too great

---

[10] Cf. *Lehrbuch*, § 93.   [11] Ibid., § 305.

[12] Beneke calls attention to this as one of his most fundamental differences from Herbart. Cf. *Lehrbuch*, § 305, note.

diffusion of these elements, the partial opposition of coëxisting heterogeneous forms, may all account for the limited span of inner conscious experience.

§ 80. *The Span of Outer Consciousness*—As in the case of inner experience the question arises, why all the infinite traces with which the soul is stored do not arise into active consciousness at once, so a pressing psychological question in respect to this system of innumerable primary powers postulated by Beneke, is why all the unappropriated primary powers of which the soul consists are not stimulated at once. A perhaps more exact statement of this question would be— why are these primary powers not all clearly represented in immediate conscious experience? Clear consciousness, however, we have seen, arises chiefly because of the simultaneous excitation of the numerous similar traces which correspond to and give clearness to any immediately stimulated primary power. Immediate sensuous experience is possible, according to Beneke, only when a still unappropriated primary power is actually entering into relation with the external stimulant.[13] If then at any given moment our field of view is restricted to a particularly narrow circle; if at any given moment, the volume of sound is less extensive than on other occasions, this is because fewer primary powers belonging to each of these systems are being actually and immediately stimulated from without. And, where this is so, the whole reason in general is that the amount of immediate outer stimulation is not enough to excite all the primary powers. As a fact of immediate observation, apparently only a certain few of the primary systems are at work at a given time. This is strikingly true in the case of sleep, where most of the so-called outer senses are almost entirely inactive. And this relation between our sleeping and waking moments is so

---

[13] "Only by means of *still unfilled* primary powers can the soul take up *immediate* imprints from without." *Lehrbuch*, § 56, note.

closely connected with the question of the span of consciousness as to call for more detailed consideration.

§ 81. *The Relation between Sleep and Waking*[14]—Beneke, in his explanation of the phenomenon of change from sleep to waking, turns to most ingenious use his distinction of activity and inactivity of the primary powers and systems. Our sleeping and waking moments are to be distinguished in general by the fact that under each of these circumstances "*various systems* of the soul's being are *active* or *aroused*: in waking moments, those senses from which the higher conscious psychical forms arise and with which the muscular system is connected, i. e., those which are capable of a voluntary movement; in sleep, the vital processes, or assimilating activities of the body, by means of which takes place the appropriation of the material consumed for their nourishment. Other systems, like the circulatory, respiratory, and that of digestion, show themselves active in both cases."[15] Beneke therefore assigns a positive and a secondary character to sleep. "The *essential nature* of sleep, or its fundamental *positive characteristic*, accordingly, is to be regarded merely as the *ruling activity of the appropriating powers of the body*. Everything else, even the discontinuance or limitation of (clearly) conscious processes, is only *secondary* and *unessential*."[16]

§ 82. *Why the Activity of Various Systems Monopolizes Immediate Consciousness*—Even though it be conceded that the character of immediate consciousness is determined primarily by that group of primary powers which is being immediately excited by external stimulants, the question still remains why at any given time the ruling activity should belong to any special group or number of such powers. In

---

[14] Cf. *Lehrbuch*, (ch. 8, II., 2): "*Verhältniss zwischen Wachen und Schlaf.*"

[15] *Lehrbuch*, § 312.   [16] *Lehrbuch*, § 312, note 2.

particular we may ask: (1) Why in waking moments the activity of the bodily powers is obviously suppressed or overshadowed by that of the higher senses, or (e. g. where one becomes so lost in abstract thought as to be perfectly oblivious of surroundings [immediate outer experience]) by that of the higher spiritual powers? (2) Why it is quite possible, at times, for the more spiritual processes, which are really the clearest or strongest (*Stärksten*) of all, to succumb to the vital processes, the faintest of all?

The first question Beneke answers in a simple way. Traces become traces by a partial disappearance of the stimulant. For a permanent existence of a trace at least *some* of the original stimulant must remain appropriated by the primary power. On the basis of the varying degrees of *completeness* with which stimulants are retained by the primary powers, Beneke assigns to the latter varying grades of activity (*Kräftigkeit*).[17] In this respect the primary assimilating powers of the body are least active of all. They therefore are the furthest removed from the spiritual powers, and "are therefore the least fitted to enter into *connections* with these. As result of which, consequently, both these classes of powers are able to operate at one and the same time with the greatest difficulty, and the assimilating powers of the body in waking moments of necessity become overwhelmingly suppressed."[18]

The answer to the second question furnishes an ingenious explanation of the phenomenon of sleep. "Active consciousness, as we have become persuaded," says Beneke, "is a complex process, for which at every moment we require new nourishment. This can be obtained for it only either by still unfilled primary powers adding themselves to it, or by means of external stimulants, the taking up of which is like-

[17] *Lehrbuch*, § 33. [18] *Lehrbuch*, § 313.

wise conditioned by the presence of still unfilled primary powers. But now for every sensuous feeling or perception a special primary power is consumed;[19] and in as much as that which is consumed is replaced during waking moments, perhaps not all or at any rate only in slight measure, a time must come in which *all* the unfilled primary powers become employed or worked up, and in consequence of this, consciousness discontinues, not from pressure of that fainter power, but *in itself.*"[20] This is why we can feel ourselves unable to see or hear, etc., and can actually perceive, or feel, sleep coming on.

§ 83. *Fourth Fundamental Psychological Process*—The attempt at philosophical explanation of sleep, as just given, points to the most hypothetical and therefore most criticised of all the fundamental psychological processes contended for by Beneke,—the formation of new primary powers. This process, given second in his list, is stated by him as follows: "*The human soul is constantly acquiring new primary powers.*"[21] In this consists the "*innermost life process*" of the soul. The nature of this process, more, even the *fact* of it, is by no direct means known to us. We can only postulate its operation as the most plausible hypothesis to account for the obvious exhaustion of certain systems of primary powers, this exhaustion varying all the way from diminished activity, such as is exhibited in the phenomena of fatigue, to absolute inability, as manifested in sleep, to form any sense perceptions or higher active psychical forms.

---

[19] Great caution is needed in understanding this expression. Beneke does not mean that a primary power in becoming appropriated *ceases to be*. The primary powers still continue to exist, but in modified form. To say that they are "used up" is simply to say that they are worked up into a structural form.

[20] *Lehrbuch*, § 314.   [21] *Lehrbuch*, § 24.

III THE NATURE AND MEANING OF CONSCIOUSNESS [22]

§ 84. *Introduction*—The desideratum of stamping precise meanings on the various uses of the term consciousness, a word also in his day open to the most varying philosophical interpretation of all, was expressly recognized by Beneke, and his attempt to meet this desideratum resulted in that most profound philosophical distinction which promises to prove perhaps the most permanent achievement of his whole psychology. This distinction, as we have seen, is that between consciousness as a *product, i. e.*, consciousness on the side of its *presented contents*—immediate experience of the individual as it lies before him open to direct observation—and consciousness as a *process, i. e.*, consciousness on the side of its *presentative activity*—an activity which, as the preceding psychological analysis has attempted to show, is involved in every individual conscious fact, whether of inner or outer experience.

A—CONSCIOUSNESS AS PRESENTED CONTENTS [23]

§ 85. *Consciousness Distinguished as Presented Contents*— The general character of the presented contents of immediate momentary consciousness, as it presents itself in the experience of the individual, the preceding analysis has already sufficiently described. The most fundamental description of the phenomena of life is that which distinguishes them into "outer" and "inner," referring the former to matter or body, the latter to self or soul. In the variegated and incessant alterations which the phenomenal conscious-

[22] For the full discussion of this subject compare: *Lehrbuch*, Ch. 3, I.; Ch. 8, II.; also *Die neue Psychologie, Sechster Aufsatz: " Ueber das Menschlichen Bewusstsein."*

[23] I have borrowed the terminology "presented contents" and "presentative activity" from Mr. Stout. Compare the article already referred to (*Mind*, January, 1889).

ness undergoes, this limited consciousness, so far as adult, readily distinguishes its experiences further into three great classes: Cognitions, Feelings, Volitions. One may become absorbed in clear sense perception, lost in deep feeling, or intently engaged in continuous action (doing or thinking). Each individual conscious state of this sort has its particular object or content. Except so far as such concepts are intuitively implied in these conscious experiences, these states do not know themselves as cognitive, emotional or volitional. It is only a *new*, succeeding or subsequent state which makes the concept explicit, that is, *knows* consciousness to have been engaged in any one of the ways described. It is through these subsequent, reflective, knowing states, becoming in their turn part of the presented contents of other subsequent new states, that we gain the concept of such a thing as an idea, and ultimately the concept of inner experience.

§ 86. *Grades of Clearness of Presented Contents*—Much of the confusion attendant on the use of the word consciousness is due to the failure to keep clear the distinction between *kinds* of presented contents, and *grades of clearness* of presented contents. So far as we intuitively apprehend particular given experiences as cognitions, feelings, or volitions, such experiences have attained to no small degree of clearness; and some particular experience thus may be decidedly clear *qua* cognition, feeling, or volition, and yet in comparison with various kinds of these great classes, decidedly obscure. Hence immediate consciousness appears to vary from states where the *whole* content is one vague undifferentiated extensive sensation (probably never existent except in the most incipient stages of infancy, and only approximated to in adult life either when consciousness is submerged in some overmastering pain, or when all clearness is removed from it by complete distraction or perplexity), through states where certain *parts*, in a penumbra of more or less clear consciousness, are discriminated as vague or perplexing sensations, to states where the contents are characterized by the most perfect qualitative clearness. It is this distinction of grades of clearness, indeed, which has become crystallized in ordinary language in the use of the word consciousness, and which is the great source of confusion respecting it. Even Beneke himself frequently lapses into this ordinary use, *e. g.*, when he says that "sensations of the soul first awaking to life are not conscious, and therefore we cannot attribute consciousness to the human soul or *an inborn faculty.*"[24] But what he must mean here, and in fact what he intends to say, is only that "consciousness," in the sense of *clear consciousness*, is not innate. Beneke, too, speaks of the later clear consciousness of the child developing itself from original "unconscious" sensations. But here again this is only a most relative method of expression, which for scientific and philosophical purposes is vicious, just because it obscures distinctions really of the utmost value for a true insight into the nature and implications of conscious life. The *obscurest sensation*, so far as it forms part of the immediate contents of some individual experience, in that it is a fact *in and for* some experiencing individual, is as truly "conscious" as the clearest sense percept or concept which ever engaged the closest attention of that individual.

§ 87. *"Unconsciousness" Distinguished as (1) Less Clear and as (2) Non-presented Contents*—There are really then two meanings which we may assign to the term "unconscious," from the point of view of presented contents.

First, as stated in the last paragraph, it may refer to perceptive (external) or conceptive (internal) facts, immedi-

---

[24] *Lehrbuch*, § 57.

ately present in conscious experience, but of so vague a character as to admit of only some such characterization as "sensation," "feeling," "external," "internal," etc. In other words, in this sense, the use of the term is purely relative, referring to more or less qualitatively clear actually presented contents.

Second, "unconscious" may refer to percepts (things) and to concepts (ideas) not present in immediate conscious experience at all. This second use calls for further careful discrimination. For these things or ideas either (a) may have already once formed part of the immediate contents of a given individual's consciousness, but at a given moment may not be present; or (b) they may have never at all entered into the conscious experience of the individual. In the first case, I may be said to be utterly "unconscious" of those of my friends who are neither immediately present to my perceptive consciousness nor are present in my thoughts. In the second case, I may be said to be utterly "unconscious" even of the existence of thousands of people whom, though they live in the same city with me, I have never either seen or heard of. There is a vast difference in the meaning of "unconsciousness" in these two cases. The last one does not and cannot even exist as a problem for the individual whose experience is thus, as to certain individual facts, regarded as a perfect blank. It can exist only for a second individual who knows both the particular facts and the condition of that mind supposed not to be possessed of the facts. The first case, on the other hand, raises what has proved one of the most troublesome questions in all philosophy—the question of the existence and nature of what has once been the object of consciousness, when that object is not actually perceived. And Beneke's general theory is permanently valuable just because of the light which it throws on this question.

B—CONSCIOUSNESS AS PRESENTATIVE PROCESS

§ 88. *Consciousness Distinguished as Presentative Activity* —Beneke gets at the very heart of the difficulty involved in the problem stated in the last paragraph by his distinction between presented contents and presentative activity. The result of the preceding psychological analysis has been to show that every momentary or substantive state of consciousness, whatever its phenomenalistic aspect may be, is to be regarded as a sort of static condition or equilibrium, resulting from the balancing or equalizing of certain elements—each pulse or alteration of consciousness being only a disturbance of the old and a readjusting to the new equilibrium. The factors of this balancing process in the case of outer perception are really three: (1) External Stimulants (*Reize*), (2) Primary Powers (*Urvermögen*), and (3) Traces (*Spuren*). In the case of inner perception the factors are two: (1) Traces[25] and (2) Movable Elements; or, (1) Traces, and (2) Unfilled Primary Powers. The immediate momentary consciousness of individual experience then, whatever its presented contents, is the direct product of certain primary powers which, together with their corresponding and connected traces, are being directly stimulated or aroused. Immediate consciousness, from this point of view, thus means only actual *excitation* (*Die Erregtheit*), that is, the immediate activity of certain psychical forms.

§ 89. *Clear Consciousness as a Grade of Presentative Activity*—We are now in a position to understand more fully the effect on the contents of consciousness of the degree of activity represented by the relation between primary

---

[25] Traces, it will of course be remembered, are supposed to be fundamentally only certain primary powers, or groups of such powers, which have appropriated external stimulants, and from which this stimulant has become partially disengaged.

powers and their stimulants. We have already described the general character of consciousness, or the constructive psychical forms resulting from the varying relation of power and stimulant. It is the purpose here to look more closely at the nature of *clear* consciousness, so far as dependent on presentative activity. The soul in its original nature or being, we have seen to be a vast system of primary powers all organically combined in one concrete whole. The simplest original sensation, that is, the simplest "appearance" in consciousness, arises only when the primary power is stimulated by means of a stimulant from without. But when once a stimulant has been taken up from without, it continues its existence henceforth as a permanent possession of the soul. It has become entirely psychological in character. This of course does not mean that it is always *clearly* represented in consciousness, but only that there always remains as a permanent possession of the soul the primary power and stimulant in a more or less firm connection. And this "permanent possession" continues to exist as a trace, having so become by a partial disappearance of the stimulant. So far as similar traces become multiplied in the soul, these traces, in consequence of the fundamental psychological processes, become closely knitted together as a group, which group, when active, becomes, on the side of presented contents, represented in consciousness as a single act. Now "the word clearness" (*Klarheit*), says Beneke, "means in general, nothing more than that which arises as product from the fusion of many similar psychical products of the same fundamental form."[26] Clear consciousness hence "develops itself out of the original sensations, without requiring anything new or foreign to be brought to it, *by virtue of the mere aggregation of like elements and*

---

[26] *Lehrbuch*, § 60.

the strengthening *(Verstärkung)* thereby resulting."[27] And Beneke, therefore, gives as his ultimate definition of clear consciousness "*strength of psychical being*" *(Stärke des psychischen Seins).*[28]

§ 90. *Grades of Presentative Activity*—In the case of the developed soul we may distinguish four important grades of activity conditioning the production or failure to produce clear consciousness:

1st. Where the stimulation is great enough to bring a certain psychical form into active consciousness, but the given form, in consequence of the fewness of similar traces, becomes in consciousness not a clear presentation *(Vorstellungsbildung),* but a mere vague sensuous feeling *(Sinnliche Empfindung).*

2d. Where, although the soul is supplied with traces of similar forms sufficient to result in clear representation, the balancing elements, or quantity of stimulants, becomes so *dispersed*[29] through the great number of parts of an interconnected group or series, that no one part is brought into clear consciousness. It is by this diffusion of excitation *(Vertheilung der Erregtheit)* that Beneke explains the distracted and perplexed states of the total immediate consciousness (or even of partial consciousness) already described.

3d. Where the soul is both furnished with sufficient traces, and the balancing elements are at work in sufficient quantity, to arouse or actively excite these traces. This is the condition of ordinary clear presentations.

4th. Where clear consciousness arises from the partial opposition of forms immediately present *in* consciousness, and reaches a certain maximum or perfect clearness. In this

[27] Ibid., § 57. [28] Ibid., § 57, note 1.
[29] Cf. *Lehrbuch,* § 93, note. Also § 161.

case the clear consciousness arises from the obscuration or darkening of forms immediately present. For example, where momentary consciousness, divided between several percepts, say a red, a white, and a blue ball, at almost the same instant, irresistibly and almost to the exclusion of the objects named, becomes focussed or centred on the concept "color."

§ 91. *"Unconsciousness" Distinguished as Non-Excitation*—We are now able to assign some intelligible meaning to that use of the term "unconsciousness," which has already been defined as the non-presence in immediate consciousness of things or ideas which "have already once formed part of the immediate contents of a given individual consciousness." Unconsciousness in this sense means simply the *non-excitation* or inadequate excitation of elements already existing and forming part of the being of the soul. Traces, whether consisting of partially stimulated individual primary powers, or groups of such powers, are "unconscious" in this sense, *i. e.*, so far as their stimulation is too slight to give them clear representation in immediate conscious experience. It thus results that the only absolute or "true consciousness" is unconsciousness in the sense of utter non-excitation, and this can be only in the case of the unappropriated primary powers. So far as "unconsciousness" pertains to the developed soul, it is only in respect to the still unfilled primary powers. "Also in the developed human soul under the usual circumstances, the still unfilled primary powers are unconscious,"[30] says Beneke. And adds, "They first become *conscious* by being filled with stimulants." The instant any of the primary powers receive stimulation, that instant the conscious experience of the soul begins.

[30] *Lehrbuch*, § 88.

CHAPTER VII

Applied Psychology—Metaphysics

§ 92. *Introduction*—Psychology was regarded by Beneke as the fundamental science, of which all the other philosophical disciplines are merely applications. These applications, to Ethics, Logic, Pedagogy and Metaphysics, Beneke has worked out with a consistency of principle, elaborateness of detail and profoundness of insight that make all his works on these subjects worthy of more careful and extended study than has hitherto been given to them anywhere, Germany included. Important, however, as all these applications are, it will be possible here to consider only the Metaphysics.

Beneke's Metaphysics was first published at Berlin in 1840, under the title: *System der Metaphysik und Religions-philosophie aus den natürlichen Grundverhältnissen des menschlichen Geistes abgeleitet.* The work is divided into three chief parts, the first treating of the definition of the relation between presentation and being in general; the second being an investigation of the forms and relations which lay claim to reality; the third being an investigation of our belief in the supra-sensible, this part being termed by Beneke *Religions-philosophie.* In the following exposition of Beneke's metaphysical standpoint, I cannot of course attempt to follow his formal argument. I can only set forth the spirit of his Metaphysics, and call attention to its chief points, with the hope that this may lead to further study and investigation.

I THE ORIGINAL NATURE AND BEING OF THE SOUL

§ 93. *Psychological Summary of the Nature of the Soul*—
If the preceding psychological analysis has taken true account of the facts of experience and been correct in its interpretation of those facts, there are certain inevitable conclusions which must be drawn as to the original nature and being of the soul.

As to this original being, the whole process of psychical development has tended to show that there is nothing innate in the soul of man except those senso-spiritual primary powers by which the outer stimulants are taken up and appropriated for the formation of sensations, and those vital and muscular powers which are like in simplicity with the faculties of sensation. We must of course regard as an innate characteristic, however, of this concrete system of primary powers, already originally organically combined, its ability to undergo transformations in accordance with the fundamental psychological processes already stated. To the primary powers, it is true, too, we must assign a twofold original definiteness of character. First, that of the particular original fundamental system to which they belong, and second, an original definiteness of character, as indicated in their varying grades of reaction on stimulants. In this respect, the various systems seem to differ originally in their grade of vigorousness (*Kräftigkeit*), quickness (*Lebendigkeit*) and irritability or susceptibility (*Reizempfänglichkeit*). The being of the developed soul differs from that of the original soul only in the more highly organized character of the interrelated systems, due to their stimulation both from without and from within.[1] Originally each of the primary powers was a blind impulse striving for its outer stimulation. When once stimulated it sinks to a trace because of a par-

---

[1] The inner character of the developed soul is thus partly self-determined.

tial disappearance of its stimulation. So far as it is a trace it is likewise a striving (*Strebung*), longing or aiming to recover its lost stimulation. Thus it results that "in the *developed* human soul, there are found *two fundamental kinds* of strivings: the *still unstimulated* primary powers, and those which have again become free through the *disappearance of stimulants*. The latter are distinguished from the first in precisely this, that they are strivings *after something* (*i. e.*, after an exactly definite stimulation). In other respects the fundamental character of both is the same; and *all* strivings arising through the disappearance of stimulants *arise finally from the primary powers given originally unfilled.*"[2]

§ 94. *Unity of Consciousness Distinguished from Unity of Being*—The unity of consciousness, now, is to be sharply distinguished from this "universal and indeterminate unity" which pertains to the original being of the soul. The soul originally is unconscious, in the only true sense of that word, but in virtue of the "inborn tendency" of the primary powers for consciousness (*eine angeborene Anlage für das Bewusstsein*),[3] we may speak of consciousness as one of the possible properties of it, and therefore ascribe consciousness to it in an *adjectival* sense of the word. There is, however, a more *substantial* sense in which the term consciousness may be used of the soul. In this sense it pertains to the developed or developing soul, and refers to that organized tissue of unconscious traces which constitutes the "inner being" of the soul.[4] By "unity of consciousness," therefore,

---

[2] *Lehrbuch*, § 168 [3] Ibid., § 57.

[4] This *developed* inner being is of course to be distinguished from the *original* inner being, or organic system of unstimulated and unconnected (*i. e.* secondarily unconnected) primary powers. If the primary power, after appropriating a stimulant, becomes a "trace" by the *partial* disappearance of this stimulant, then in the *developed* inner being we have power and stimulant still in combination, but

we may refer either to the unity of the presented contents of the *clear momentary experience* (or some particular percept or idea forming part of that content), or to the unity which would be possessed for consciousness by the whole mass of accumulated conscious forms, if these forms by adequate stimulation of the whole system of powers of the soul, were all simultaneously presented as clear consciousness.[5] But the important point to notice is that whichever way we conceive it, unity of consciousness is always to be distinguished from the original being of the primary powers, howsoever dependent it may be on the latter.

§ 95. *The Soul a Concrete Psychical Organism*—With Beneke, therefore, the soul is neither a *tabula rasa*, nor a transcendental unity, somehow pre-furnished with certain original "forms" or "categories," by "stamping" which on the raw sense-material fortuitously furnished it from without, it constitutes experience. Not a *tabula rasa*, because the character of sensation is determined by the nature of the appropriating primary power as well as by the irritating stimulant. "The human soul in the case of no process is purely passive; even for the production of the liveliest sense impression is a species of *activity* necessary on its part."[6]

with the difference that the strength of stimulation is not sufficient to make the given psychical form, or sensation, (or rather what *would be* the sensation or the presented contents, if the stimulation were sufficient), enter *clearly* as part of the contents of clear consciousness. There is no objection to or contradiction in speaking of this combination of power and stimulant as inner "consciousness," if we bear clearly in mind the meaning of consciousness as "process," varying in grades from full excitation (*Erregtheit*) to complete non-excitation (*Nicht-Erregtheit*).

[5] This aspect of consciousness, dealing with "Reality" as distinguished from "Being," appears to be the ultimate standpoint of those thorough-going empiricists who confine themselves to what Kant called "nature as a totality of objects of experience;" for example, Mr. Lewes, in his "cosmos of experience," and Mr. Spencer, in his phenomenal world of "the knowable." How Beneke transcends this point of view, the text shows.

[6] *Lehrbuch*, § 23, note 2.

Nor a being stored with *preformed* "categories," because the forms of intuition and the categories are but logical distinctions *for consciousness*, and as such are but the *content* of an idea in inner experience.[1] Objective validity in a certain sense they have, but not objective existence, or rather *being* in and for themselves. So far as they have being, their being is to be found in the being of the particular concepts of which they are the content. And as to concepts, the whole preceding psychological analysis has tended to show that of these "*there are absolutely none inborn.*" Their being then is nothing apart from just those particular primary powers in whose connections and stimulation the concept consists, and of which it is the "presented content" aspect.

The soul, therefore, according to Beneke, is a concrete psychical organism whose activity in consequence of stimulation from without manifests itself in the form of conscious experience, and this experience for the developed soul distinguishes itself into a twofold aspect—outer and inner.

II THE NATURE AND LIMITS OF KNOWLEDGE

§ 96. *The Intuition of Self*—From what has already been said it is obvious now that we must distinguish sharply the true self from the *knowledge* of self. The true self Beneke regards in a twofold aspect: first, as the undeveloped being or self, which consists in the original systems of primary powers organically combined, which original combinations or relations are the only permanent or unchanging relations of the soul; second, as the "concrete Ego," which, in consequence of its constant stimulation from both without and within, and the new connections and relations thereby established within it, changes with every momentary experience.

[1] " Even the so-called *categories* or *pure* concepts of the understanding of Kant show themselves, on deeper examination, as having been formed from intuitions, and as presentations of our own self-consciousness." *Lehrbuch*, § 122, note 2.

It is with this latter concretely developing self that our knowledge endeavors to keep pace; but so far as we know it, we apprehend it in a *concept*, which, in its *being*, is only a small portion of the total being of the soul, but which, in its *reference*, is the refined essence of the whole rich manifold of our preceding conscious experience, outer and inner. The intuition of self, therefore, is no innate concept, in the sense that we are equipped with it at the start in life's journey through experience. It is a concept which only gradually and after a long attentive process builds itself up as a permanent possession of our inner consciousness. This concept, too, to be true, must be developed by the experiencing individual himself. While the concept of self as an outer and inner conscious experience combined in the organic unity of a personal being may represent the high-water mark of philosophical speculation, only those individuals who have reached this intuitive insight through a long reflective process on their own experiences, by which they have mounted step by step and higher and higher from an obscure sensuous basis to this clear spiritual insight, can be said to have, in any true sense of the word, such an intuition of self.

§ 97. *The Origin and Content of "Inner Sense"*—The concept of experience as an outer and inner form of consciousness, that is, as appearances to a perceiving self, represents a very advanced stage in the evolution of knowledge. And since in inner sense we seem to get nearest the soul itself, we may now inquire how this faculty of inner perception has grown up. That it has grown is not lacking in evidence. How long it took human consciousness to reach the phenomenalistic conception of itself, such as it attained in the idealism of Berkeley and the empiricism of Hume, is a matter of philosophical history. How possible it is for a person to perceive objects, experience feelings, or perform actions, without ever being in the slightest degree conscious of these experiences *as* perceptions, *as* feelings, *as* volitions, is a matter of every-day experience. Children see and hear, remember and pass judgment, yet in the early periods of their career they are never conscious of their particular experiences, *as* perceptions, *as* memories, *as* judgments. In other words, "inner sense," in the strict sense of perceiving certain of one's experiences as inner, does not exist for them. They have no perceptive faculty for their own soul's development. How then is this formed, and, as a concept, what is its content?

Inner sense perception, in Beneke's view, is nothing more than a distinction *for* consciousness. So far as we *know* memories, concepts, judgments, inferences, *as* memories, concepts, judgments or inferences, in other words, *as facts of inner experience*, we have already abstracted from the contents of certain original experiences and brought into clear consciousness particular "aspects" of these experiences. These "aspects" constitute the contents of a new *concept*, which in its turn may through further reflection be conceived as a fact of inner experience. Now any original sense experience, if repeated a sufficient number of times in precisely the same way, will give rise to a concept, the concept being that apperceptive mass of similar traces, which, on the repetition of the original experience, rise into active consciousness and give it clearness. The like elements in various concepts, by a process of mutual attraction, transference of movable elements, and sufficient repetition, give rise to other higher concepts, and just such a concept as this is the faculty of inner sense. It originates in the coalescence of the similar elements in subjective forms. "Inner sense arises in the *concepts* which *refer themselves to the psychical qualities, forms and relations*. If those concepts which have as their content the clear presentation of these qualities, etc., become particular experiences for consciousness, they themselves thereby become, on the side of consciousness, so strengthened and cleared, that these particular experiences become *intuitively perceived* (*vorgestellt werden*). Consequently, as well in the case of *inner* perception, in its complete formation, as in that of outer, we find essentially the same fundamental form as that which gave itself a very distinct stamp in the case of judgments. That is, the particular feelings, strivings, etc., take, in this case, the place of the *subject*, and the *apperceiving concept*, or *inner sense*, the place of the *predicate*."[8]

§ 98. *The Soul the Only Being Known in Itself*—We are now in a position to see what is the most fundamental outcome of Beneke's psychology, and, as such, the foundation stone of his Metaphysics—*the soul is the only thing in itself of which we have absolute knowledge.* Beneke agrees with Kant that both forms of experience, outer and inner, are appearances, or phenomena, in the sense that they are both the *product* of two sets of factors. But as *process*, external perception and internal perception are radically different. External perception distinguishes itself by the presence of what is, as it were, a foreign element. That is, an external presentation is the product of the primary power and *elements outer to the soul* (*Reize*), whereas an internal presentation is the *product of elements wholly within the soul.* "In the case of inner perception," therefore, "not only the *being* of that which is taken up and intuitively presented is *attained to* by the perception or intuition, but *this being enters immediately into the presentation as an ingredient*, and in consequence of this latter, *there is added qualitatively not the slightest thing* which was not also already contained in the being intuitively presented."[9] This is the ground, then, for Beneke's claim that in inner perception, in inner experience, we have "a presentation *of complete or absolute truth.*"[9] The soul is the only being which we know in and for itself.

[8] *Lehrbuch*, § 129.   [9] *Lehrbuch*, § 129, note 4.

III KNOWLEDGE OF BEINGS OTHER THAN SELF

§ 99. *Fundamental Starting Point*—If the fundamental question for metaphysics is the definition of the relation between presentations and the beings which they are believed to represent, then, in the insight that we ourselves are a being in the apprehension of which, in inner sense, perception and being coalesce, without the admixture of any foreign element, we have a sure fundamental metaphysical starting point. "*We are ourselves a being;* and consequently we do not need, in order to reach being (*das Sein*) to go *out of ourselves* into something else. Here we have or rather are *perception and being at once*, and consequently are able to compare genuinely and with complete satisfaction the perception with its being."[10] Beneke, even in one of his earliest works, gave a sharp and clear statement of this point. He says:[11] "To every act of perception, we saw, even though it were a perception of a perception, there belongs, as an activity of the human soul, an *existence* in this soul; this is so undoubted a fact for universal human consciousness that it cannot be denied even by the most obdurate skeptic. If, consequently, it were possible for us to be always limited to mere acts of perception, at least in this act of perception itself we have *a being* incontestably within our power. But this act of perception we are able to perceive again without any difficulty; and consequently there lies before us not merely a being, but also the comparison of it with one and the same act of perception that perceives it, and, therefore, the knowledge of the relation between perception and being lies open in at least one instance."

§ 100. *How Knowledge of the Existence of Other Beings is Attained*—But now, if in outer perception our percept always

---

[10] *System der Metaphysik*, p. 75.
[11] *Das Verhältniss von Seele und Leib*, p. 42.

contains a foreign element to which we cannot reach in itself, how can we know even of the existence of other beings besides ourselves? Why are not the outer world and outer beings mere phantasmagoria of my own imagination, and I the only being that exists? Knowledge of external being "would indeed be utterly impossible, and our sensations and sense perceptions of the outer world would remain purely subjective things, if the two classes of perceptions which we have, *sensuous* perceptions and those *of our own self* (or of being), were given *entirely without connection one with the other*. We should then of course in the case of the psychical processes, which we call sensations and perceptions of the outer world, have a *feeling different* from that in the case of our other psychical processes; it would *feel different in that case* to us; but *without our knowing how to explain more precisely this difference;* and, consequently, in spite of this difference, they would never become for us perceptions or representations."[12]

But man is more than a soul; he is also a body, and this body has its representatives among the phenomena of external perception. Therefore "there is one being, of which we have at *one and the same time both kinds of perceptions*. This is our own being. We perceive ourselves at one time *immediately* through *self-consciousness* (through which originally the concept of being arises, and through which *alone* it can arise), and in addition we perceive ourselves *sensuously:* our figure, the tones of our voice, etc., in a word, all that we call *our body;* and these two kinds of perceptions (or feelings) become associated together from the first moment of life on, and continually grow in the course of life ever more intimately united."[13]

As to that particular group or series of external percep-

---

[12] *System der Metaphysik*, p. 79.   [13] *System der Metaphysik*, p. 79.

tions we have learned to call our own body, Beneke asks, why we class only a particular group with ourselves and relate them to ourselves as our body? One group of phenomena in the picture before us we call another man's body, another group we call our own. And yet originally in and for themselves external sense perceptions have no predisposition either to appear as perceptions of things in themselves, or to show any particular connection with our internal sense perceptions. The reason is to be found in the fact that those perceptions which are foreign to our own being sometimes are given in consciousness and sometimes not, and unceremoniously change without any reference to our own circumstances. On the other hand, however, "the sensuous impressions and perceptions which we class with ourselves, *are continuously present to us, and change themselves parallel with that which our self-consciousness places before us.* Originally and in itself the bond of connection between the form of our hand, the tone of our voice, etc., and our inner states had not the slightest superiority over the bond of union which occurs between these states and the form, the noise, etc., of a waterfall which we perceive and feel accidentally coëxisting in one single instance. But this latter connection becomes dissolved again, or at least does not grow up to a high grade of strength, whereas, on the other hand, the former through a thousand and ten thousand-fold repetition rises to the highest grade of strength; and only in this way, *very gradually*, the perceptions and feelings of our own body present themselves from out the assembled throng of others as one *specific* thing. They become this entirely by virtue of the intimate association brought about by an endlessly repeated coëxistence."[14]

§ 101. *The Being of Other Men*—Here, then, in the sen-

---

[14] *System der Metaphysik*, pp. 80–81.

suous perception of our own bodies, have we the basis of our method for transcending external phenomena so as to reach the being of other existences. And this method, Beneke claims, is entirely that of analogy. In inner perception or experience the soul knows itself in and for itself, it attains to its own being; in outer perception or experience, there is at least one phenomenal existence, its own body, whose being it is able to appreciate; since the close similarity of another man's body to our own can be a matter of immediate experience, both bodies occurring simultaneously, as phenomena in outer conscious experience; by analogy we conclude that his body is representative of a being like that which we know to underlie our own body. "Man, *just because he is man*, cannot apprehend and intuitively perceive in complete truth any other being than a *human* one. *Complete* truth, indeed, requires complete agreement between the perceiving act and the being perceived; and consequently only so far as our being reaches, common perceptions reach to *complete* truth. What we may perceive as metaphysically true, that must we be able to *become*, and whilst we are perceiving it, must *really become or be* it. Therefore then the province of this act of presentation metaphysically true extends to, besides our own soul's being, only the being of the souls of other men *most like unto ourselves*. All that lies without this province we are able to represent to ourselves only either by *analogies* (similes) with the human soul, or by the *effects* which it produces on our senses: in the first case, therefore, by virtue of what is given in our own being in perfect unanimity with the *foreign being*, in the second case, by virtue of a certain *entrance* into our soul of what originally was outer."[15]

§ 102. *The Being of Material Things*—Further, therefore,

[15] *System der Metaphysik*, pp. 123-24.

in respect to the existence of material things, so far as we descend in the scale of organic existences more and more unlike our own, so far are we decreasingly unable even analogically to represent these to ourselves in their inner being. While usually we are prone to assign more objective reality to our external perceptions of material things, because of their greater clearness, we must not forget that, as the preceding psychological analysis has made out, this superiority in clearness is really grounded purely *subjectively*. Since internal perceptions can gain an even greater clearness, it is a mistake to regard the substratum of external perceptions as the only *truly real*, or a "being in the highest sense of this word." We must conclude then that "the presentations of material things are only *appearances*, to which of course a *true* being or a *being-in-itself* corresponds, but which we are able to comprehend *at best only incompletely* and by analogies more or less close and enduring. We have of them no being-yielding-knowledge, (*An-sich-Erkenntniss*), but merely a *knowledge of effects*, *i. e.*, a knowledge by means of those processes which the imprint of the thing *in connection with our faculties of perception and sensation*, causes to arise in us. These products, consequently, or the intuitions of material things, exist *as such* only in us; and we are able in no manner to resolve them into their factors, so that we might be able to apprehend the real which is without us in its complete truth or in its in-itselfness."[16]

§ 103. *The External World, so far as Concerns our Fellow Beings, Neither Unknown nor Unknowable*—Thus, while so far as material things, in the sense of lower organisms, inorganic matter and chemical atoms, are concerned, we may have no adequate knowledge of the supra-sensible, it is not true that the external world, in the sense of meta-phenomenal

---

[16] *System der Metaphysik*, p. 120.

being, is entirely unknown and unknowable to us. *In the knowledge of the existence of our fellow creatures, we have a knowledge that is at once profoundly and scientifically grounded on immediate experience, and yet which transcends that experience.*

IV GOD AND IMMORTALITY

§ 104. *Introduction*—The third main division of his *Metaphysik* Beneke terms *Religions-philosophie*, as having to do with such suprasensible being as constitutes the peculiar object of religion. A distinguishing characteristic and a radical departure of Beneke's Metaphysik in this respect, is its relegation of the question of the freedom of the will to Ethics as a purely scientific and empirical question. This question, as well as that of the cause of evil, and the means of removing it, " have to do through and through with *what is given in experience*, or with *facts*, and these allow themselves to be completely understood and treated in accordance with the *natural laws* of *our own soul*."[17] The two chief questions, therefore, to be considered concern God and Immortality.

§ 105. *The Existence of God*—In his treatment of the existence of God, Beneke shows most the influence upon him of Jacobi, and the "Glaubensphilosophie." So far as the object of religion is the suprasensible, in a sense differing from our fellow beings and similar beings, to this we can only approximate in that most highly developed subjective state of feeling called conviction or faith. This feeling " can acquire the highest certainty of conviction; but we *cannot objectify it, i. e.*, with complete truth perfect it as an object of our knowledge."[18] Beneke, therefore, in summing up the matter, says: "Of only a single class of existences are we able to

---

[17] *System der Metaphysik: Vorrede*, xi.   [18] *Metaphysik*, p. 565.

gain a completely clear and profoundly comprehensive knowledge—human souls. Of everything else, whether it be ever so near us and be given in manifold ways, we apprehend first of all only the superficies, or appearance, not its inner being, its own individual existence; and however we strain our faculty of knowledge, we are able, in respect to these latter, to form nothing further than an obscure and indefinite analogy with our own being. Beyond the whole province of what becomes immediately given or presented to us, there opens up besides the unending realm of the non-presented (*Nicht-Gegeben*): (from the lowest being) up to the Being of all beings, the Author and Ruler of all that exists. But of this realm still less are we in a position to know: not through our knowledge do we attain to it, but our flight thereto must be reached from another side, from the side of emotion, which gives us wings in Faith and Hope."[19]

§ 106. *Immortality*[20]—Beneke's doctrine of the immortality of the soul is perhaps one of the most profoundly scientific attempts at the resolution of this problem ever put forth. It promises not an immortal atomism, but an immortal personality. It has its basis entirely in his scientific psychology.

Beneke attempts first to answer the question, what is natural death? We have come, in the preceding psychology, to regard the soul as an organic system of primary powers, and to postulate that for every outer sensuous impression a special unfilled primary power of the soul is used. For the existence of these primary powers two hypotheses are possible. Either the entire number necessary for the

[19] *Metaphysik*, pp. 598-99.

[20] Compare *Lehrbuch*, Chap. 8, IV: " *Von den innersten Grundformen des Lebens und des Todes.*" Also, *Metaphysik*, Part III, Section 2: " *Die Fortdauer der menschlichen Seele nach dem Tode.*"

whole life of an individual is already and originally given at birth, or, the soul has the power to form ever anew fresh like powers. We have had to postulate, as the innermost life process, the continuous production of new primary powers. Now we have seen how all psychical processes tend to remain in the inner being of the soul as traces, and how, in the course of life, this inner being gains in increasing richness. We have seen, too, how by unnumbered repetition these traces not only gain in strength and in intimacy of union, but, with this increased strength, require less stimulation either by external elements or internal stimulants, to become aroused into clear consciousness. The child and the youth seek ever new sensations and stimulation from without, the activity of the man is rather spent in reproducing and working out the assembled mass of previously gathered experiences. As life progresses, then, in consequence of the activity of the soul being turned more and more upon its inner self, the formation of new powers becomes *limited*. In consequence further of this limitation of the outer life of the soul, the concentration of the psychical processes upon the inner being mounts higher and higher. A time then must come when the formation of new powers like unto the primary ones either entirely ceases, or is not sufficient to produce enough powers to maintain the usual span of outer consciousness. Outer consciousness consequently ceases, and this is natural death.

As to the continued existence of the soul after death, a psychology *grounded entirely on experience* of course can present only conjectures. But this psychology has tended to show that death, in the natural sense, is a *daily process*. The more highly organized a man's inner consciousness becomes, the nearer he approaches natural death. Death, then, is not a *dulling* of the inner powers, but rather a "continuous strengthening of the inner upbuilding." The essential aspect of death is to be found in the destruction of the coherence between the inner being of the soul and the outer world, upon which, of course, during the progress of our earthly life, the *conscious* developments of our soul have been dependent. Consciousness, therefore, must cease, too. But the *inner* or *more spiritual consciousness*, which has arisen on the original basis of sensuous experience, has become a permanent possession of the soul. If, then, the soul have a continued existence hereafter, for the excitation and further perfection of its inner organization, there " would not, perhaps, be necessary *again a new sensuous system*, but merely *such environment* as would have the power to make active or consciousness-producing those powers (*Vermögen*) which were founded in this life and have become unconscious traces or elements tending to produce active consciousness "[21] (*Angelegtheiten*).

[21] *Metaphysik*, p. 460.

CONCLUDING CHAPTER

I BRIEF CRITICAL ESTIMATE

THE most important general characteristic of Beneke's philosophical system is its remarkable combination of sound common sense with profound metaphysical insight. This alone, not to mention its admirable clearness of statement, ought to commend the system to all English philosophical students. It has been justly said of the system, too, that it begins and ends with experience. This is only a brief way of paying tribute at once to its profoundly scientific character, and to its value for practice.

Whatever may be said in criticism of detailed points of this system of philosophy, I believe it will be some day generally conceded that Beneke has made four cardinal and permanent contributions to philosophical theory. These may be summarized as follows:

1. *In internal sense-perception we are able to know ourselves, not as a phenomenon, but with complete metaphysical truth.* In the insight that the only being we truly know, *i. e.*, know in itself, is that of our own soul, Beneke marks his great advance on Kant. As Beneke himself claimed, in the knowledge of the being of self we have for "in-itselfness," for true being, a clearly defined standard which can guide us with its clear light through all the other labyrinthine paths of metaphysical discussion.

2. *Consciousness or knowledge is to be clearly distinguished in its aspects as clear presentation or appearance, and as presentative process.* In its former aspect, it must be regarded in the

case of external perception, as the product of objective (or "external") and subjective factors; in the case of internal perception, of subjective factors entirely. When, therefore, it is asserted that we know our own soul's being, this means, not that we have an innate idea or intuition of self, co-extensive or identical with our soul's complete organic being, but that in these entirely derived forms of knowledge or consciousness discriminated as facts of inner sense or experience, neither of the component factors is "sense-material" in the Kantian sense of a foreign element from without, but both factors are psychical, that is, both are ingredients or parts of our own soul's being.

3. *In consequence of the distinction of unity of consciousness from unity of being, the individual soul or self must be regarded, not as an undifferentiated abstract unity, but rather as a concrete psychical organism, consisting in various subsystems or organic groups of primary powers.* The demonstration of self as a concrete system of distinct but organically interrelated parts, arrived at by a purely empirical method, is a valuable achievement.

4. *In the knowledge that back of the external perceptions called our own body there exists a true psychical being—a being in itself that is directly known to us—we have an analogical but valid means of escape from a purely subjective idealism.* In internal perception we know ourselves as a psychical being. In external perception we know ourselves as a corporeal being. Through this twofold knowledge of self we are able to transcend self and get at the existence of like beings.

These cardinal contributions to philosophical theory, moreover, result in a general metaphysical conception of the individual self or soul that is particularly valuable as offering a rational and satisfactory explanation of many vexed psychological and philosophical questions. While it will be impossible to take up the consideration of these questions here with any detail, I should at least like to call attention to the particular significance of Beneke's theory for such problems as the association of ideas, subconscious mental life, latent mental modifications, and the general doctrine of evolution.

While Beneke is a thoroughgoing associationist, with him, as the preceding text has attempted to show, it is not ideas that become associated. That is, ideas in the sense of the qualitative details of the presented contents of conscious experience. Ultimately it is not sensations that combine to make up the complex of adult conscious experience, since sensations themselves, even if realizable, would be only *appearances*. It is the underlying *factors* of sensations that become associated. Moreover, the mooted problem, if such an inconceivability can be called a problem, of how a series of events could ever become conscious of itself as a series, becomes fully and rationally provided for in the organic unity which must be conceived as already belonging to the fundamental elements of the sub-systems of the soul and to these systems as a whole. Matter too is scarcely to be defined as a mere "permanent possibility of sensation." A mere possibility is nothing. Matter is something truly real, and so far as it exists in an organic form approximating to our own bodily organism, we have some true knowledge regarding its nature.

Beneke's general theory of the self throws valuable light, too, on the psychological problems of subconscious mental life and latent mental modifications. Both these problems involve the nature of *retention*, that is, the nature of supposed facts not immediately present in conscious experience. They therefore are insoluble except on a metaphysical basis, meaning by this some general conception of the nature of conscious experience as a whole. It is usual to interpret retention in either of two ways. The first interpretation conceives retention as the *continued existence of an idea*, AS AN IDEA; the second, as the *mere psychological persistence of a modification of nerve structure*. Beneke's general conception, while precluding either of these as ultimate interpretations, embodies the partial truth of both. The usual objection to the first interpretation is that if all experience is to be regarded as a form of consciousness or knowledge, then it is a contradiction in terms to speak of an "unconscious" or even a "subconscious" idea. An idea is essentially a form of consciousness. But this rigid insistence on terminology ignores the common ambiguity in the uses of the term consciousness. Beneke meets this objection in his distinction of varying grades of presented contents, and also in the insistence that it is not qualitative content as such that is retained, but primary powers and stimulants in a more or less durable connection. This last statement reveals the basis of what would be his objection to the purely physiological interpretation of retention. Nerve structure and nerve process are not the ultimate facts. Nerve structure is known only so far as *perceived*. As perceived it is a *phenomenon* in some individual conscious experience. As phenomenon it is the product of objective and subjective factors—the external stimulants and the internal primary powers. These stimulants or these powers may become structurally "modified," but this is a different thing from making retention a modification of nervous structure *as known*.

Finally, Beneke's general theory is of peculiar value for the general doctrine of evolution. It has been acutely said of Mr. Spencer's valuable contributions to this doctrine that almost all of what is said on this score would be equally true and valuable on a metaphysical basis entirely and radically different from that furnished by the synthetic philosophy. In the synthetic philosophy the lack of adequate appreciation of the true metaphysical problem always has been, and will be, the stumbling block to its full acceptance. In Beneke's theory we have a most thoroughgoing evolutionary conception combined with the profoundest metaphysical insight. Evolution may be, and doubtless is, both an individual and a cosmical process, but in either case it is one which takes place in an essentially psychical being, that is, in a being which exists primarily in and for itself, and which is already originally an organic unit.

It is not to be inferred from what has been said above that Beneke's system is without defects and not in need of any further supplementing. His most serious metaphysical defect, perhaps, is in assigning a qualitative difference to external stimulants, and yet regarding these not only as entering into connection with the primary powers of the soul, but as being actually transformed into psychical elements, and thus being made permanent possessions of the psychical organism. The logic of the situation, however, is such as to lead, not to the rejection of Beneke's view, but rather to the extension of his conception of organism to include all being. This, however, is not to identify the individual with the cosmos or God, whichever we chose to call all being, any more than, for example, the system of primary powers constituting the sense of sight is to be identified with the whole being of the individual self or soul possessing it. Both are distinct differentiations of the total organism, both are centres of activity determining the action of and being determined by the action of the whole. The true source of the conception of organism is mind, not matter.

II PERMANENT INFLUENCE AND FOLLOWERS

A word now remains to be said as to Beneke's permanent influence and principal disciples. This influence, which, for accidental reasons already in part pointed out, has been chiefly pedagogical rather than either psychological or philosophical, it will be convenient to speak of first as regards Germany itself, and then as regards other lands.

It is scarcely too much to say that in Germany, Beneke's philosophical influence has been almost *nil*. The two chief reasons for this have been, on the one hand, the overwhelming weight of Hegelianism; on the other, the preponderating influence of the Herbartian Psychology. And yet it is not far from the truth to say that this eclipse of Beneke's philosophical standpoint has been the direct result, not of a fair contest, but of injustice and misrepresentation. The unjust attempt, originating in Hegelian sources, to stifle Beneke's thought, has already been sufficiently pointed out. The equally unfair attempt to dispose summarily of Beneke's psychology as well as of his pedagogics, as a mere modified Herbartianism, has likewise been shown to be ungrounded, although it has since been perpetuated by numerous writers. Perhaps the only more distinctly philosophical work largely influenced by the thought of Beneke is that of C. Fortlage, whose work Ueberweg speaks of as "a compound of Beneke's empiricism and Kanto-Fichtean speculation with independent modifications." Fortlage's chief works are: *System der Psychologie* (Leipzig, 1855); *Psychologische Vorträge* (Jena, 1868), and *Philosophische Vorträge* (Ibid., 1869).

On the pedagogical side Beneke's influence has been much greater. The most prominent among his pedagogical followers, and the man who has done most to elucidate, defend and extend his thought, was Johann Gottlieb Dressler[1] (died 1867), one time director of the Seminar in Bautzen. Another name that deserves always to be associated with Beneke is

[1] See Bibliography.

that of Dr. G. Raue, whose exposition of the outlines of Beneke's psychology (*Die neue Seelenlehre*, already referred to as afterwards enlarged and extended by Dressler) did perhaps more than anything else to popularize his system among teachers. Others who made various applications of Beneke's principles to the theory of education are mentioned, with the titles of their works, in the bibliography which follows.

Outside of Germany, Beneke's work, while not unknown, has so far exerted no appreciable influence. In two comparatively recent and important psychological treatises in America,[1] Beneke in one case is not even mentioned; in another, he is dismissed in a few sentences. A third work[2] shows considerable traces of Beneke; but with a tendency to reflect the undue emphasis of Beneke as scientific pedagogist only. In England, too, attention to Beneke has been slight. Sully[3] avails himself of some of Beneke's pedagogical results. The only real attempt in the English language at a serious study of some of Beneke's results, has been the paragraphs on Beneke in the article in *Mind*, by Mr. G. F. Stout, already referred to. In France, M. Ribot, in the first edition of his *Psychologie Allemande Contemporaine*, called attention to the neglect of Beneke in Germany, but gave only a meagre exposition of his system. His attempt, therefore, as reproducing the letter rather the spirit of Beneke, proved unsuccessful, and so was withdrawn from the second edition.

[1] James: *Principles of Psychology* (2 vols., New York, 1893); Ladd: *Elements of Physiological Psychology* (New York, 1888).

[2] Dewey: *Psychology* (New York, 1893).

[3] *Outlines of Psychology* (New York, 1893).

III BIBLIOGRAPHY

1. LIFE—The chief and almost only source is Diesterweg's *Pädagogisches Jahrbuch für* 1856. In this is contained, besides an excellent portrait of Beneke, first, a short comment by Diesterweg; second, the fullest account of Beneke extant, by Dr. Schmidt; third, a valuable biographical addition by Dressler. Of the summaries in the histories of philosophy Ueberweg's is the best (pp. 282–283, Vol. II). In some of his own writings, however, Beneke has left an interesting record of his intellectual development, particularly in *Die neue Psychologie* (Berlin, 1845), third essay: "On the relation of my Psychology to Herbart's." The brief memorial, *Kant und die philosophische Aufgabe unserer Zeit*, is very valuable as showing his relations to contemporaries. Fortlage, in the fourth of his *Acht Psychologische Vorträge* (Jena, 1872), "On Character," turns aside to pay a glowing tribute to Beneke.

2. WRITINGS—Many of Beneke's writings are hard to procure, no complete edition of his works having ever been published. The bibliography in Ueberweg (pp. 283–86, Vol. II.) is very complete. The most complete and best list is that of Dressler, given as a supplement to the fourth edition of Beneke's *Lehrbuch der Psychologie* (Berlin, 1877); also published separate. Its value lies in its being also: "A Brief Characterization of the Complete Writings of Beneke, in the order of their publication." For Beneke's writings not mentioned in the preceding text consult these sources. Deserving of special mention, however, since so far Beneke's influence has been greatest in the field of education, is his *Erziehungs und Unterrichts-lehre* (2 vols., Berlin, 1835 and 1836).

3. EXPOSITIONS OF THE SYSTEM—Of the general expositions of Beneke's philosophy in German histories of philosophy, by far the best, since the most complete and apprecia-

tive, is the most recent, viz., that of Julius Bergmann, in his *Geschichte der Philosophie* (Berlin, 1893): Vol. II., "*Die deutsche Philosophie von Kant bis Beneke,*" pp. 544–583. Ueberweg's exposition (History, Vol. II., pp. 281–292) is a good summary for one already familiar with the spirit and method of Beneke. The account by Dr. Albert Stöckl, in his *Geschichte der neueren Philosophie von Baco und Cartesius bis zur Gegenwart* (Mainz, 1883), Vol. II., pp. 258–282, is valuable for a certain fulness of exposition, but particularly as showing at once the nature and impotence of the hostile criticism directed against Beneke. The account by Falckenberg (*op. cit.*), while brief, is excellent.

Besides the above-mentioned general sketches of Beneke's system, a thorough and complete popular exposition of his psychology has been made in German by G. Raue, in *Die neue Seelenlehre Dr. Beneke's nach methodischen Grundsätzen in einfach entwickelnder Weise für Lehrerbearbeitet* (Bautzen, 1847); later editions, including the fourth (Mayence, 1865) edited by Dressler (Translated into Flemish, by J. Blackhuys, Ghent, 1859; into English, Oxford and London, 1871; also into French, says the Encyclopedia Britannica). A most complete popular summary of Beneke's whole system is that by Dressler in Diesterweg's *Pädagogisches Jahrbuch für* 1856, pp. 33–105: "*Ueber Beneke's Forschungen.*" A complete epitome of *Die Lerhbuch der Psychologie*, preserving so far as possible the sentences of the original, has been made by Gustav Hauffe, under the title "*Professor Dr. Eduard Benecke's Psychologicals Naturwissenschaft,*" Borna-Leipzig, (vi. and 116 pp.). For a good exposition of Beneke's educational standpoint see Lange's revised edition (Köthen, 1876) of Dr. Karl Schmidt's *Geschichte der Pädagogik:* Vol. 4, article 37, pp. 1059–78. (Translated into English by Louis F. Soldan, *Journal of Speculative Philosophy*, October, 1876.) Compare also: *Die Unterrichtslehre*

Beneke im Vergleiche zur pädagogischen Didaktik Herbart, by Otto Emil Hummel (Leipzig).

In English no independent investigation of Beneke's complete work exists. So far as his psychology is concerned, however, we have a brief critical and expository account in an article by Mr. G. F. Stout: "Herbart compared with English Psychologists and with Beneke." (*Mind*, January, 1889.) His educational views are set forth in Barnard's *Amer. Journal of Education*, vol. 28: 54; vol. 24: 54.

For *M. Ribot's* attempt to resuscitate Beneke, compare the first French edition of his *Psychologie allemande contemporaine*.

4. WORKS OF BENEKE'S FOLLOWERS—Beneke's followers have extended his system and its principles mainly in the field of education. The most prominent is Johann Gottlieb Dressler. Besides the works already mentioned, he published: *Beiträge zu einer bessern Gestaltung der Psychologie und Pädagogik*, also entitled *Beneke oder die Seelenlehre als Naturwissenschaft* (Bautzen 1840–46); *Praktische Denklehre* (Ibid., 1852); *Ist Beneke Materialist? Ein Beitrag zur Orientirung über Beneke's System der Psychologie, mit Rücksicht auf verschiedene Einwürfe gegen dasselbe* (Berlin, 1862); *Die Grundlehren der Psychologie und Logik* (Leipsic, 1867, 2d ed. by F. Dittes and O. Dressler, 1870); and numerous contributions to pedagogical journals, particularly Diesterweg's *Pädagog. Jahrb*.

The following list of other writers largely influenced by Beneke is given on the authority of Ueberweg, Dressler, and the article on Beneke in Richard Lange's revised edition of Dr. Karl Schmidt's *History of Pedagogics*. J. R. Wurst, in his *Die zwei ersten Schuljahre*, applies Beneke's psychology to the theory of education; his *Sprachdenklehre* derives its didactic form from Beneke. Kämmel, on the basis of Beneke doctrines, made numerous contributions to Hergang's *Pädagog. Realencyclopädie.* Other writers of Beneke's school are: Otto Börner, *Die Willensfreiheit, Zurechnung und Strafe* (Freiberg, 1857); Friedrich Dittes, *Das Aesthetische* (Leipsic, 1854), *Ueber Religion und religiöse Menschenbildung* (Plauen, 1855), *Naturlehre des Moralischen und Kunstlehre der moralischen Erziehung* (Leipzig, 1856), *Ueber die sittliche Freiheit* (Leipsic, 1860), *Grundriss der Erziehungs und Unterrcihtslehre* (Leipsic, 1868, 3d ed., 1871): Heinrich Neugeboren and Ludwig Korodi, who published the *Vierteljahrsschrift für die Seelenlehre* at Cronstadt from 1859 till 1861; F. Schmeding, *Das Gemüth* (Duisburg, 1868); also Ueberweg, who is frequently classed with the school of Beneke on account of his prize essay— *Die Entwickelung des Bewusstseins durch den Lehrer und Erzieher (Eine Reihe pädagogisch-didaktischer Anwendungen der Beneke'schen Bewusstseinstheorie, besonders auf den Unterricht an Gymnasien und Realschulen.* Berlin, 1853).

VITA.

Francis Burke Brandt was born in Philadelphia, June 13th, 1865. His early education was received in the public schools of that city. In 1880, after a two years' course at the Central High School, he left to enter business. In 1888 he entered the Brown Preparatory School, Philadelphia, and the following year was admitted to Harvard College. Here he specialized in philosophy under Professors Royce, James, and Palmer, and Dr. Santayana. He was graduated from Harvard in 1892, after a three years' course, with the degree A. B., *magna cum laude*, and "honorable mention" twice in philosophy (*in philos. (bis) excellentem*). He also had conferred on him at graduation "honors" in philosophy (*in philosophia* HONORES), in recognition of special examination and a thesis—"The Relation of the Kantian Philosophy to the Problems of the Present Day, and the Permanent Influence of this Philosophy as a Criticism of the Powers of the Human Reason, both Theoretical and Practical." For two years after graduation he was instructor in English and Mathematics at Columbia Grammar School, New York City. During this period also he pursued graduate studies under the Faculty of Philosophy, Columbia College, attending advanced courses in philosophy and education under Prof. Butler, and performing experiments in educational psychology under Prof. Cattell. In April, 1894, he was appointed for the succeeding academic year University Fellow in Philosophy at Columbia College. During the term of his fellowship he continued his studies in education and engaged in original research in German philosophy under the direction of Prof. Butler; attended the seminary of Dr. Hyslop; and studied sociology under Prof. Giddings, of the Faculty of Political Science.

www.ingramcontent.com/pod-product-compliance
Lightning Source LLC
Chambersburg PA
CBHW030243170426
43202CB00009B/613